FAST-PITCH SOFTBALL
FUNDAMENTALS

*A Collection of Essays and Reflections on
Coaching and Playing
by
Coach Dick "Smitty" Smith*

Wish Publishing
Terre Haute, Indiana
www.wishpublishing.com

LCCN: 2003112648

Edited by Kathy Sparrow
Editorial assistance provided by Amanda Burkhardt
Cover designed by Phil Velikan
Cover photography NYD

Printed in the United States of America
10 9 8 7 6 5 4 3 2 1

Published in the United States by
Wish Publishing
P.O. Box 10337
Terre Haute, IN 47801, USA
www.wishpublishing.com

Distributed in the United States by
Cardinal Publishers Group
7301 Georgetown Road, Suite 118
Indianapolis, Indiana 46268
www.cardinalpub.com

ACKNOWLEDGEMENTS

To say that my wife, Ruth, helped with this work is an understatment of grand proportions. She cheered me on, made me laugh and goaded me into completion of the task. Without her, this work would not exist; nor would I.

My wonderful son, Ernie, and a marvelous mutual friend of ours, the late Bob Drazkowski, planted so many seeds of learning, thought and understanding in my store of knowledge, that without them the larder would be empty.

Further, the enumerated trio spent hours editing, reflecting and relentlessly critiquing me, my thoughts, typing, spelling and general demeanor. Blank pages would have resulted without their help, love and devotion. I thank them for that and for being my friends. Who needs more than that?

TABLE OF CONTENTS

An Introduction:
HOW DO YOU SPELL SUCCESS?

To be successful coaches, we must teach our players the little things which go beyond the normal textbook stuff describing how to hold a bat, the stance, ball grip, etc. What counts is the attention to the little details of the game. Textbooks are fine, but how many times do we need to be told how to hit by writers, plus the myriad of clinicians, who all pretty much say the same thing in an agonizingly redundant and commonplace approach?

I in no way wish to demean these people, for their efforts are necessary, commendable, and the methods are usually correct. What is missed are the little, subtle details that go along with, and into, the grip, the stance, the throw, the catch, and all the other game adjuncts.

Success includes the "little things," and they begin with truth and the real meaning of athletics. Few are the athletes that go on to greater rewards in the professional ranks. Many are those that leave the athletic arena and go about their daily lives, rarely returning to organized competition. What they take from the athletic arena is generally directly related to what we as coaches have given them during our brief associations.

Personally, I would prefer that my players leave not only with the best coaching I can give them, but with the knowledge that they have assimilated the coaching and done the very best job that they can possibly do, wins and losses to the contrary notwithstanding. In other words, play the game hard, fast, and as well as you can. Treat opponents, associates, and others in a fair and truthful fashion. Learn from your mistakes, and apply the lessons learned to the next game and, subsequently, to your life. Finally, enjoy what you are doing or go play checkers, or whatever.

Success is difficult to define, but somewhere I read what it is in the eyes of a baseball coach. He said that success is seeing one of his players come back wearing a three-piece suit, sitting down, and reminiscing about the good times past.

SMITTY SAYS:

Play the game for what it's worth. Play it the right way. Play it hard, giving your best. Whether there be victory or defeat, players and coaches should relish the shared experience of a unified effort. And consider it a blessing that you were able to play, for there are those who cannot. Success, then, is spelled, as you would have it.

The definition of success cannot be confined to the final victory. If it were, then there would be an enormous number of unsuccessful teams since there is only one winner at the final moment of truth. So, am I to believe that all those who came in second or worse were unsuccessful? I think not.

My measure of success is simple: If I am crying at the end, then the season was a success. If I can't wait for the season to be over, it has been a failure. No other criteria come to mind.

Still, the team might have a winning season, but there are downcast heads when it is all over, because of team turmoil, discontent with the coach, or a feeling that one's child did not get a fair shake.

Winning seems to be the sole measure of success for most, as it pertains to the team as a whole. But if the team had a losing season and, for example, one player played exceptionally well, the general feeling of the team will be quite low, while that of the successful player might be the opposite. It all depends upon whose gourd is being oxed, if I may coin a phrase, for what is success to some often is failure to others and vice versa.

Part One:
IN THE BEGINNING

Chapter 1
WHAT IT TAKES TO BE A GREAT SOFTBALL PLAYER

To be good at anything, it takes hard work, long hours, practice, patience, proper attitude, and a willingness to learn. Softball is no different than anything else. True, it is just a game, and mostly it is played for fun, but it still takes lots of hard work to be good at the game. Few are willing to do what it takes. So what does it take?

There are those who are handicapped and cannot play the game as others do. They should not be denied the opportunity to play within their capabilities. This essay does not apply to these folks. It applies to those who have their physical and mental attributes intact and who desire to reach the pinnacle of success. Coaches, it's up to you to convey the following to the best of your ability. To do so, will ensure that you will have a team of players ready to take to the field.

To begin with, an athlete's body must be in condition. A swimmer cannot expect to succeed in swimming the English Channel unless she has prepared for it. The same applies to softball. Here we start with the basics, even before setting foot on the field — a healthy diet.

A proper diet means simply good eating habits. If a player is overweight, or even slender, she should consult a doctor before starting any diet. Even if she appears to be slender, she may have too much body fat. It pays to get it checked out.

Good eating habits mean three meals daily, plenty of liquids, especially water and juices, plus food from the basic food groups. There are scads of books available today on diet, some written by professional athletes and noted experts in the sports field. They're well worth reading.

But to get started, remember that sweets and fried, greasy foods are to be avoided. Fresh fruits and vegetables are vitally important. Get your players to learn to love their veggies.

> **SMITTY SAYS:**
>
> *Becoming a great softball player is not an accident. It is the result of hard work, dedication, and love of the game.*

Encourage players to "carb-up" before a game, with such foods as pasta and baked potatoes. But remind them to eat lightly at least two hours before a game. Lots of water is important before, during, and after any competition in any kind of weather.

Proper rest is a must. Many folks these days are sleep deprived. Growing bodies need plenty of rest, eight hours is recommended. It also helps the body to have a routine by rising and retiring at the same hour each and every day.

Training is yet another important factor in getting an athlete's body into condition, and this includes correct exercise and stretching. All athletes need to learn how to stretch the right way. Exercises include calisthenics and running, lots and lots of running. Pitchers and catchers should jog for long distances. Other players should do less jogging and more sprinting for short distances. Swimming is very good. Weight lifting should only be done under proper supervision.

Softball training includes proper warm-up before practices and games. Have players jog until they break a sweat. Then have them spend five to 10 minutes stretching. Then sprint short distances for two to three minutes, followed by overhand throwing for another 10 minutes. This warm-up may take as long as 20 to 30 minutes. Don't fudge on this aspect. To do so courts disaster, not only for individual players, but the team as a whole.

After the warm-up, players practice the skills that pertain to their particular area of the game. This would include pitching, infield and outfield drills, and batting practice. Pitchers must work very hard for many years to perfect their skill. Other aspects of softball, such as fielding and hitting, do not take as much time as pitching, but still, the more players practice, the better they will be.

Some say Ted Williams was the greatest baseball hitter of all time. He used to take batting practice until his hands bled. When he was asked what would make him a better hitter, he said, "More batting practice." Think about that!

Many kids these days need a good attitude adjustment. Some softball players are amongst them. A good player must have a good attitude and a desire to be a team player. Everyone gets in a sour mood now and again, that's a part of human nature. But overall, positive attitudes must abound.

Players should not only want to win, but also learn not to get down on themselves when the team loses or they have a bad game. To be a really good winner, a player must always believe in herself, her team, and her coaches. She must learn to be a good loser, too, for there will be many defeats in a softball career, and she must know how to handle them.

A good player must also be willing to accept discipline, have a desire to learn, and the ability to have fun. These are essentials!

Further, she must also comprehend what her coach wants. If she does not know, she must be encouraged to ask for clarification. Coaches, tell your players to speak up if confusion settles over the playing field.

Hustle is very important. And this does not mean simply running fast. It means sprinting very hard from here to there or wherever. It means chasing foul balls, picking up bats, balls, and other equipment. A good player will help her coach and teammates with whatever needs to be done. She must be willing to warm up the pitcher when the catcher isn't ready and volunteer to go to the bullpen to catch pitchers. Encourage players to put some zing into their step. Sprint to and from their position. Show their passion by simply loving the game and being happy and proud to be a part of a great sport.

And that includes coming to the practice field to practice and the playing field to play. When a player hits the field, tell them to do it with enthusiasm, and a willingness to work hard. Encourage them to come to games ready to play, with fire in their heart, and a desire to do the very best that they can. The same goes for you, coach.

There will be many problems along the way to becoming a great softball player. Players may have problems with their parents, coach (if you can believe such a thing), and even some teammates. Their game may go sour from time to time. The team may be on a losing streak. Fans may get on their case or nerves. They may have aches and pains or an injury that plagues them relentlessly. Many may have jobs or activities that are the cause of fatigued or unhappiness. All these things, alone or together, can make a player want to quit the game.

But real athletes, those that want to be the best, overcome these problems. They learn to deal with them on a case-by-case basis, and do not let them mount up over long periods of time. If they can learn to deal with these problems in a logical way, they will not only be prepared for softball, but for larger problems that crop up later in life.

Chapter 2
PRACTICE MAKES PERFECT

Softball practices are, oh, so typical. Players do some stretching, running, and then they play catch, after which coach hits some grounders and fly balls. Sometimes there is some practice on bunt defense or other aspects of the game. Practices last usually, from an hour and a half to three hours, depending upon how much the coach talks. Much of the time, players stand around doing absolutely nothing.

There is the apparent feeling that hitting a few grounders and fly balls will do the trick. Repetition will do the teaching and make great players, or so it is thought. No doubt about it; practice makes perfect.

All this is fine for well-tuned and skilled players who execute everything right. And we all know who these players are, don't we? Olympic athletes, perhaps, but few others, very few. One of the very first games in the new women's professional league included a fine display of how not to play the game, so it is clear that even the best have problems with fundamentals.

That's why the professional baseball leagues and winning softball programs have specialists in various areas of the game. These people hang around, seemingly doing nothing, but in reality they are very busy. They are watching for fundamental faults that tend to creep into the actions of even the very best players. They are the fine tuners, the coaches who teach, the ones who hone the skills of athletes and keep them sharp.

The lower the level of softball, the more teaching is required, but unfortunately, the better coaches are at the upper levels where it is thought the athletes need only have their skills honed. Whether this last is accurate depends upon one's perspective, since many professional athletes are woefully lacking in fundamental skills. Yes, the virus of imperfection is rampant in sports.

SMITTY SAYS:

In the olden days, kids often gathered up a bunch of rocks about one inch in diameter, tossed them into the air and hit them into a field using a broomstick, and it was done by the hour. This was great for hand-eye coordination and it developed good hitting techniques. Since houses have replaced our cornfields, kids today could use a one-inch dowel rod, or a broomstick, and some golf ball-size whiffle balls. The drill can be done almost anywhere, even at those tournaments where they don't allow batting practice. It gives players lots and lots of swings, and cannot help but improve hitting, especially if a coach is standing by to correct faults that creep into the swing.

The therapy is in teaching correct fundamentals along with repetition. Pure repetition will not cut the mustard, though, because if players are doing it the wrong way, they are merely engaged in the practice of making errors when fielding and outs when batting.

For example, the soft toss is a fine hitting drill, if done correctly, but it seldom is. Usually a player receives tosses in quick succession and then swings, and swings, and swings. There is rarely anyone standing by to watch and make needed corrections. Whatever hitting faults exist are reinforced with each swing and will, without fail, be carried to the plate.

Let's assume a player hits an inordinate number of fly outs, and the reason is that her hands allow the bat head to drop. During a toss drill a coach must correct the fault, else it will be reinforced with each swing.

There is a hitting drill using a long pole with a ball on the end. A coach imitates a pitch by bringing the ball into the hitting zone and a batter attempts to hit it. One can observe as many as 50 swings being taken and not one word of instruction offered. Although the player is getting a lot of exercise, if her swing is imperfect, her outs will be consummate.

Hitting grounders and fly balls is necessary and nice, but if routine practices are observed, there is usually little or no instruction during drills. Bad fielding habits previously acquired are merely reinforced. Errors in the making!

Now, it is not always easy to see an athletic fault. It takes a trained eye to see these things, and then it takes a coach who knows how to teach in order to correct defects. Coaches need to obtain the necessary skills to see and repair these faults, and then to sustain the proficiency of their athletes. Experience helps, but this takes time and comes at a very high price. Clinics are beneficial, as well as talking to others about ideas and techniques. Books and tapes are available, too.

Sometimes, we cannot see the trees for the forest, and a stranger to the team can spot something we cannot. But, because of pride, stubbornness, or ignorance, coaches are sometimes reluctant to seek out advice from others. This is a fatal defect in coaching.

There are conditions where even superior coaching methods and efforts come up short. There are some athletes who are uncoachable, either by design or because they cannot perform certain athletic feats.

Every team has a variety of players, many of whom are very good athletes. But each team also has a variety of player types. There is Miss Ideal who will not listen because someone has told her how great she is or because she doesn't like the coach. There is Miss Inept who will try very hard, but does not possess many athletic abilities. There is Miss Congenial who is a good athlete, but her mind cannot comprehend what a coach is trying to teach. Then there is Miss Clueless, who is forever gathered unto a cloud of nothingness. No matter how smart a coach is, no matter how great that coach is as a teacher, no matter the coach is a fine person, it is a real challenge to train these types of players. Practice may not be of any benefit.

All coaches want the kid with the great attitude, who is a hard worker, has athletic ability, and who responds to coaching. We need no law for this type of player. She is pure pleasure to have on a team.

But no matter the character or condition of your players, you must still practice them and do it correctly. Even the best players will not reach their potential without the kind of practice that bears the perfect label. Yes, practice must be perfect. The instruction must be perfect, and the execution must be perfect. Practice, itself, does not make perfect. Perfect practice will not always guarantee perfect success on the diamond either, but percentages say your odds of success go way up using this approach.

Chapter 3
Trials and Tribulations of Indoor Practices

So, you've no place to practice in the northern climes, eh? Well, don't feel like the Lone Ranger. There are scads of teams vying for gym space when the weather will not permit us outdoor activities. Most are basketball or volleyball teams, and such ingrates do not look kindly upon a bunch of softball ruffians trying to bring an outdoor sport into their arenas. They offer us little sympathy. So off we go to find somewhere to work our charges, lest we be left behind in the softball "race."

But, not to worry. All is not lost. We can do a great deal of work in very limited space. No, it's not the same as being outside, and our limited space will never afford us the luxury of full field practices, but at least we can work on some fundamentals.

We must remember that even when a gym is available, we are limited in time as well as space. Most coaches do not use time well, so it's necessary to be really organized. If we only have a short time in the gym, perhaps we can stretch out and get our sprints in somewhere nearby so that when we enter the gym we will be ready to go to work.

If no gym is available, try to locate an area such as a hallway, a classroom, a basement, or a garage. Even though the type and extent of our practices will be dictated by the size of our practice space, there are a ton of things we can work on in such small areas. A hallway, for example, will tolerate whiffle ball batting practice and base running drills.

You can set up a miniature diamond in a small area and use a make believe ball, which I call a "magic ball," and work on situations, backups, etc. This ball costs nothing and won't break anything. You can even have an infield practice and hit magic fly balls to your fielders. They can learn drop steps, how to round off fly balls, and how to handle obstacles. They can work on do-or-die plays, backups, and all manner of softball activities. You are limited only by your imagination.

An area measuring a few feet can accommodate short hops, reaction drills, relays, rundowns, holding runners, run-through throws, short tosses, double play pivots, force play footwork, tagging runners, plate coverage by pitchers, catchers' blocking drills, pick-off plays, hustle drills, bunting, footwork, leadoffs, diving, flip or soft toss drills with whiffle balls, and perhaps a whiffle ball game with short bases.

Limited space also provides an opportunity to have skull sessions where you go over defensive coverage of bases, signals, defenses, offenses, situations, scouting reports, charting pitches, team assignments, travel, motels, conduct, and other team matters.

A classroom provides an opportunity to show videos of games, hitters, fielders, pitchers, and techniques used by major league baseball players. Blooper videos are great, not only for entertainment, but to show kids that even the best players make mistakes, and that there are ways to correct the errors.

There are many fine teaching videos on the market that players can watch. Many of these show aspects of the game that can be taught in limited space. For example, kids can view a slap bunting video and then practice the technique in a hallway using a whiffle ball.

In the "olden days," I was forced to practice my teams inside prior to our southern trip. Each year we played teams that not only practiced outside, but which had already played several games. A disadvantage? Of course, but the indoor practice, sometimes in limited space, always paid off.

Inefficient use of that precious commodity, time, is a tragedy, but it is prevalent. Coaches are often seen hitting ground balls, one at a time, to a line of several players. This may go on for a long time, with each player getting only a few balls. This is a colossal waste of time. If space permits, two or more lines should be set up. If there are not enough coaches, use players to hit the balls.

Actual productivity can be increased if coaches would simply roll or bounce balls to players, rather than hit them. This is much faster and each player will receive many more chances. Instead of getting five grounders, each player may get 20. If coach wants to really challenge the players, then a bat can be used to hit the balls harder. Just don't have kids standing around!

SMITTY SAYS:

Coaches should have a bag of balls with them during fielding drills. There is nothing worse than having to wait for a player to chase down a ball she has missed, retrieve it, and then get it back to the coach. If a player misses a ball, let it go and hit her another. If she misses that, hit her another. She can retrieve the balls after the drill is over. Having players needlessly track down balls that have decided to elude fielders often wastes valuable practice time.

Drills can also be used as conditioners. For example, set up Line 1 of about five or so kids. Set up Line 2 about 20 feet away with three kids, Line 3 another 20 feet away with three kids, and a catching station with three kids. Roll a ball to the first line. The first player in line fields the ball and throws it to lead player in Line 2, then following the throw, she moves to the end of the line. The receiver pivots and throws to the player leading Line 3, then she follows the throw, and takes her position at the end of that line. Line 3 receiver pivots and throws the ball to the catching station, also following the throw and moving to the end of the line. The catcher rolls the ball to the Line 1, then following the throw, gets last in line. If kids sprint to their various stations, they will get tons of practice and after five minutes will be a pretty tired group.

The imagination is great if used. If you put a little thought into your practices, you can come up with some wonderful drills. The idea is to work kids hard in the short time you have them, not allowing them to loaf. Correctly using your time with the team will vastly improve your chances of having a successful season.

Remember, the size of the galaxy is astronomical. Our practice space is not. Use it efficiently.

Chapter 4
It Might Be... It Could Be... It Is!
A New Season

Ah! Fancies in the North turn to so many things in the Spring, one of which is softball. Some teams practice inside during the winter months, or in the case of those out West or in the South, have held their sessions, including games, outside. Nice, this being able to play outside and develop fundamental skills year round. But those in the northern latitudes must await the garaging of the snow plows to hit the playing field.

Thus, the arrival of Spring is a wonderful coming, for it is then that the less fortunate experience high school play. Can the summer travel team be far behind? Coaches, players, and fans await the arrival of the playing season with a high degree of anxiousness and wondrous expectations, albeit there is a certain amount of trepidation involved.

Misguided folks think victory should be the goal in the coming season. Ha! If you focus on that as a goal, you will fail to attain it, for victory is not a goal. It is but a consequence. It is the result of the correct execution of fundamentals, plus a little luck along the way. Now what's this foolishness all about?

Well, let's see. What's involved in the game of softball? There is pitching, hitting, running, sliding, fielding, and throwing, along with some brain gymnastics. If these things are a given, then shouldn't our goal be to execute them correctly? Yes, indeed, we must takes steps to employ them properly.

To begin with, our players must be in condition to play. Girls coming off athletic seasons such as basketball are generally in pretty good shape. The others will report to us in a dreadful state. Poor conditioning leads to all manner of complications, such as injuries, illness, muscle and skeletal problems, as well as performance failure.

Our first function then is to try to get our charges in shape. Our practices must be geared to do this. Proper stretching must be a focal point, for this facet of training is often ignored or given a mere passing glance.

Each coach will have to determine what is needed in the way of conditioning. Perhaps a trainer or physical education teacher could be invited to the first couple of practices to help educate both players and coaches. Keep in mind, there are many practice drills which can double as conditioners, and this will save practice time.

Running, especially short quick sprints, is an integral part of the game, and cannot be ignored. Unfortunately, players on many teams have incorrect running forms which, more times than not, cost dearly during games. Practices might include the local track coach to give your players at least the basics in the fine art of running. You will be amazed at the results.

Just as there is more than one way to skin a cat, although I have never had the occasion to accomplish that feat, there are many ways to to throw a softball. Examples include the backhand flip, the run-through, the pivot throw, the underhand throw, the long throw by shortstops and outfielders, the crow hop, the relay throw, and the overhand flip. All must be learned and practiced. Merely playing catch for a few minutes before practice or a game does not sharpen the knife for the cat.

There is a great deal more to fielding practice than hitting a few flies and some grounders. Often this is the extent of training on teams. Players must be taught proper techniques to field fly

---

SMITTY SAYS:

Coaches and players must certainly be aware that there are clinics and camps out there, all over the place. Some are quite good and offer an opportunity to learn. If we are to improve in any area, we must always be ready to seek out new ideas and to try them out. If the new is unworthy, then we must practice and use the old ways, for most are tried and true. Harvey Penick, the great golf teacher, said words to the effect that if he stopped learning, he would stop teaching. Sound advice for any coach.

balls and grounders both backhand and forehand. The jab and drop steps need a ton of work. Players need extensive practice in charging ground balls and looking the ball into their gloves. Then there are short hops, hot grounders, and liners. All these and more need drilling, drilling, and more drilling.

Obviously, pitching and hitting practices are required for any successful team. Most teams spend a great deal of time on these essentials. Sometimes I wonder if other parts of the game suffer because of an inordinate amount of time spent in these areas. Clearly, they are important, but we must make sure not to short-change all else.

Sliding seems to be part of the game oft neglected. Signs of poor techniques can be seen at every game — bloodstained uniforms, limping players, and those on crutches nursing torn ligaments and sprains. Many of these ill-fated tragedies can be prevented, and in the process we might see a few more safe calls.

Brain activity is a matter that is difficult to control. Players either have field and game sense, or they don't. It cannot be practiced or taught.

Preparation for the season is a must. That is a given. We cannot just throw our players and expect them to walk away with the booty. It will do until the other teams catch up and then watch out. Ever see an "all world" team win, win, win, and then suddenly their efforts begin to fail, fail, fail? Sure you have. You see, the other teams have been working hard on fundamentals and have soared by this gaggle of high-flying geese.

It is not by accident that certain players make the great plays time and time again, year in and year out. They have worked hard and perfected the necessary skills involved in the game. Rigorous practice and dedication have paved the way to the softball "holy grail."

Somewhere I heard or read that in order to win, we must prepare to win. Preparation is accomplished at practices. But the players are not the only ones who need to make ready. Coaches must also prepare to prepare. To realize the dream, the result, the victory, we must all be prepared, players and coaches alike. Will we be, or will we say, "It can't be....it shouldn't be...oh, merciful heavens, it is. It's a new season."

Part Two:
FANCY FOOTWORK

Chapter 5
"Da Feet" Equals Defeat

In Chicago they say "Da Bulls, da Bears," when referring to teams, and "da feet," when talking about those items attached to their ankles.

Football coaches will say, "Move da feet." They mean that one should be quick.

Basketball coaches also refer to quickness. Quickness usually refers to the first step that a player takes, providing an edge over an opponent.

"Da feet" are no less important in softball, although few coaches grasp this concept. If footwork is ignored "da feet" will often translate into defeat, a condition not welcomed in coaching circles.

Yes, footwork is directly related to fielding, throwing, and running. It plays a big part in pitching and batting, as well, but not for the same reasons.

Many college scouts pay strict attention to a potential recruit's footwork. Sluggish footwork eliminates many players simply because it slows them down during play. Remember, softball is a game of speed; speed to bases, speed in fielding, speed in swinging a bat, and speed in pitching.

Well, coach, it's been said before, but is worth repeating. Why don't you get a track coach to give your kids some running instruction? You have all year to work on this aspect of the game. You don't need a diamond, a gym, or a track. All you need is an area about 30 yards long.

If your kids learn how to run, it is an absolute guarantee that you will score more, field more balls, catch more flies, reach more bases safely, raise batting averages, and win more games.

So why don't you do it, coach? If you would work on this aspect of the game, you might just avoid explaining 1-0 losses, why your team can't field, or why your batting averages are so low. Otherwise, you have just blown it by not teaching your kids one of the basics.

SMITTY SAYS:

To be really quick on the field, players must practice every day on running and footwork. There are fun drills and games like hopscotch to help them become great players. Yes, coach, pay attention to "da feet" so dat yur yutes don't suffer no defeat.

But knowing how to run fast is just one aspect of our softball preparations. We need to learn how to prepare to run quickly.

Let's take fielding. The quicker the feet move and get the body in position, the quicker one will be able to use speed to get to a ball that has been hit. No question about it. So, it becomes imperative that players learn drop steps and jab steps to accomplish this feat.

Since mathematics kept me from becoming a rocket scientist, we must use a simple calculation that is easy to understand. A ball traveling at 60 miles per hour moves at 88 feet per second. If a third baseman is positioned 44 feet from home plate expecting a bunt, but the batter hits away instead, hitting a pitch at 60 mph toward her, the ball will reach her in a half a second. That is not much reaction time, but most experienced fielders can handle it. It becomes a so-called routine play.

But wait! That's a routine ground ball. What about a hard hit ball? What if it's going 90 mph? Now it gets serious, no? At this point the slightest hesitation by your fielder will result in the ball happily bounding into left field for what is known as a base hit. What could be an ERA-lowering play now becomes a liability to your pitcher's stats, not to mention the potential harm to the team's record.

The same occurs when a rocket is hit in the gap or over an outfielder's head. A crossover step which not only delays "da feet," but creates a bad angle to the ball, often turns a single into a double or worse. What might have been a catch suddenly turns into a serious problem for your team. In other words, incorrect techniques by your fielder inhibits her capability in making a proper fielding play. "Da feet" are the culprits.

Now, we have talked about the jab step and the drop step. What are they? The drop step is a deep step taken to the rear as a ball is hit. The jab step is a short drop step. If the ball is hit long, the player is able to continue using a good angle to the ball. If the ball is short, the player pushes off the drop or jab step to move forward. If done correctly, only perfectly hit balls will fall between fielders. You will note that all good fielders will use these techniques. Just watch them.

Proper techniques will increase your fielders' range and turn ordinary fielders into great ones. Will the drop step hurt occasionally? Sure. Once in a while a ball will fall in front of player because she has made a drop step, but then it will only be a single. But a misplayed fly ball, going deep...oh, my!

As to the fine art of flinging the old softball, other than a run-through throw, one's lead foot must be on the ground before a throw can be released. Simply put, the longer the stride, the longer it will take your fielders to throw. A short, quick stride will give your fielders a faster release. Again, "da feet."

"Da feet" also come into play when hitting. Yes, they are used to hold you up, but the longer it takes to stride, the longer it takes to hit the ball. Only the "slappers" can hit with a lead foot in the air. Everyone else has it on the ground. As in throwing, the longer the stride, the longer it will take to swing at a pitch. Pitchers just love batters who take big strides. Rare is the long strider able to hit a good pitcher. Again, quick feet with a short stride or no stride at all will help your batters..

Jumping rope is an excellent training tool for all players, especially fielders. Running through tires like football players is also good for foot movement. Shadow drills, where one player mimics another, are very good, as are all dances and aerobics. These fun things will help your players move more efficiently on the playing field.

Chapter 6
FIRST BASE IS FIRST

Time is a critical factor in most sporting activities, regardless of the presence of a game timepiece. Football has a game clock, as does basketball and other sports, but softball does not. A stopwatch is used in the game of softball, because we measure time to test speed in getting from hither to yon, or in this particular discussion, from home to first base. To be on base one must first get on base. That's obvious, or is it? Sometimes tall woody plants get lost in the thicket, or words to that effect.

Let's look at time. A mature female runner, at full speed, can advance at roughly 20 feet or more per second, meaning she can move between bases in about three seconds. Some do it faster. Some slower. A delay of a mere one-tenth of a second means a difference of two feet. Two feet!

Having timed many high school batters from home to first, I find that most right-handed batters make it from the box to the base in around three and half seconds. That is from contact with the ball to contact with the base. Again, some players are faster and some slower.

My observations have led to the conclusion that there are an enormous number of times batters are out by an eyelash or even a step or two. This translates to anywhere from a few inches to five feet or so. If our math is reasonably correct and the observations are on the money, we know that in terms of time, we are dealing with between one tenth and three tenths of a second.

Think about it. One tenth and three tenths of a second are the difference between reaching first base safely and trotting to the bench. So how can we assist our batters in their effort to get on base? Easy. Cut down the running time. Even if we can't make them better hitters, we can teach them ways to get to first base more often. Well, maybe it's not so easy.

Believe it or not, for players 12 and up, the distance to first base is thought to be 60 feet. Not quite! It is but 58.75 feet! Why?

Because the distance is measured from the rear of home plate to the outfield side of first base, and the base is 15-inches wide. How can we use this fact to help our teams?

Many batters take a batting stance in the rear of the batter's box. This puts the rear foot as much as 62 feet from first base. That distance can be drastically reduced if a batter will move the back foot forward to a point even with the front of the plate. This puts her back foot about 58 feet from first. Fear not that she will be out of the batter's box when she strides, for the box extends four feet in front of the middle of home plate. Just think! By doing this a batter will be as much as four feet closer to first. Four feet!

Even though it makes sense to start near the front of the batter's box, coaches fear the aspirin tablet pitchers and think that their batters will have more time to look at pitches if they are farther back in the box.

Such thinking is true, but the time gained by batting from the rear of the box can be measured in mere microseconds. I believe that this is miniscule compared to a profit of four feet gained by being up front in the box.

As an aside, batters near the front of the box gain another advantage, which concerns breaking balls, risers, drops, curves and off-speeds. When up front, one has an opportunity to hit a ball before it completes its movement, which may be in any one direction or it may meander in various routes on its pilgrimage to the plate. This obvious benefit to the batter needs no further discussion.

Next comes movement out of the box. Coaches should take a look at the manner in which batters get out of the box after hitting a ball. Most have a very slow start because of poor balance. Their swings, for example, may pull them away from the target. A great deal of time is lost here. Work on this balance aspect, coaches. It will pay dividends.

Once out of the box, how do hitters run? Watch to see if they immediately break to the foul line. If so, they have lost valuable distance, because geometry tells us that a straight line is the shortest distance between home and first. Fear not that batter-runners will not be in the three-foot box, located 30 feet from first. This only becomes a problem when a batted ball is behind the player,

SMITTY SAYS:

Of course, the team has done sprints during training and pregame, right coach? We wouldn't want to forget to teach our players how to run and then give them some practice at it, would we? Sprinting is an integral part of the game. Curious that this aspect is commonly ignored by coaches.

and she somehow interferes with the throw or catch at first base. Otherwise, she's allowed to run in fair territory all the way to the base. This will cut down considerably on the time it takes hitters to reach their objective.

Our math course also tells us that a zigzag run to first will take more time than an outright straight-line dash to the objective. Need I say more?

Next, we should observe how our runners touch first base when running out an infield play. Most hit the middle or rear of the base. Both contacts are farther from home plate than the front of the base. Yes, the distance lost between the front and the rear of the base can be a whole foot or more! Think back, coaches. How many of your runners have been out by a step?

So, now we are going to actually have our runners try to hit the very front edge of the base, which is good. But if they miss the base, that's bad. Not necessarily. The rules are clear. If a runner misses first base, it becomes an appeal play, and that must be made before the runner returns to the base. More often than not, no appeal will be made in time, if at all. Secondly, the umpire frequently has a difficult time seeing whether or not a batter-runner actually hits the front of the base. On appeal, good umpires will give the benefit of a doubt to the runner, unless the violation is clear.

There are times, however, when a batter-runner might trip over the front of the bag. This is a definite possibility and does occur. However, hitting the top or side of a bag has its pitfalls, too. Sprained ankles and knees often result. And when one steps on the side of first base, there is a tendency to peel off toward the right, thus taking the runner farther from second base in the event of a misplay at first. We do teach our runners to "run through" the bag, do we not?

Finally, the first base coach is often treated like a third thumb...necessary, yet superfluous. Are they? Well, it is another of Smitty's Laws that requires a first base coach to be just that: a first base coach! If that person is on the ball, first base will be a more common terminus than the bench. Let's get to first base first.

Chapter 7
Obstruction, A Season Ender

While watching or participating in softball games during the erstwhile, I have had occasion to evaluate a disturbing trend. It has to do with obstruction, a defensive rule violation. Now, before we get started, let it be known that there are aficionados of the game who will strongly disagree with certain of these discoveries, subsequent conclusions, and recommendations. But be that as it may, here goes.

Obstruction is defined in the rule book, but violations are often difficult to enforce. It is an easy call when it rears its ugly head right in front of an umpire, but if it occurs away from the action, it is often missed. Even if obvious to all, umpires might either not know the rules, be unwilling to enforce them, see the action differently than the coaches of the offended team, or they might be just plain incompetent. In any case, the violation is a tough call.

The urge to win at all costs often dictates unfair practices and highly illegitimate methodologies that simply must not be allowed on the field of play. Here are some examples:

Situation 1: Runner on first attempts to steal second base. Second baseman, having already positioned herself near second, steps into the base path as if to receive the throw from the catcher. However, the throw is actually going to the shortstop who is covering the steal. Upon seeing the second baseman in her path, the runner is obligated to do one of three things. She can go around the baseman, slow up, or make contact. All three situations normally result in an out. This is a clear case of obstruction, but the defense will claim the second baseman was going for the ball, and thus there was no defensive obstruction. Amazing!

Situation 2: Runner on first leading off on a pitch. The first baseman is "cheating" toward the bag. As the ball is pitched, the runner leads off, and the first baseman moves into the baseline between the bases, about three feet away from the bag, thus block-

SMITTY SAYS:

Obstruction is an act that heralds a season ending injury. We don't need that. There are enough dilemmas in coaching without asking for trouble. Ponder this for awhile, coaches.

ing return access to first base. Note that the defensive move is prior to any play on the runner. Next, the catcher throws to first for a pickoff. The runner is blocked and the out is made. The defense claims the baseman was going for the ball and so there was no obstruction. Remarkable!

Situation 3: Runner on second in a steal situation. The shortstop positions herself in the baseline between second and third bases. As the runner breaks for third, the shortstop moves slowly ahead of her in the baseline, thus impeding the runner's direct line to third base. The catcher makes a soft, lob throw to the shortstop. Seeing the shortstop in the way and depending upon how close the two are, the runner will either slow down, go around the shortstop, or make contact with the fielder. Again, the claim will be made that the shortstop was going for the ball. Astounding!

Situation 4: Runner in scoring position. A ball is hit that will advance the runner to home plate. Immediately after the ball is hit, the catcher moves into the baseline between home and third base, three or more feet up the line. If the play is not going to be close, the catcher merely steps out of the base path. Otherwise, the catcher will straddle the foul line and prepare to catch the ball for a tag. The runner has the same options as in two of the situations above, none of which will benefit her. The defense will again claim that the catcher was going for the ball, and there was no obstruction. Incredible!

If we really analyze all four situations, obstruction began even before the play began. Think of it! What can we coaches be thinking about? Is placing our kids in harm's way good coaching?

Now before you get all upset with me and tell me that catchers and others are allowed to block bases, think of the consequences.

Runners moving at roughly 20 feet per second can cause unimaginable damage to themselves and to fielders who intentionally get in their way. Collisions can be frightful, devastating, and season-ending. This is true for both offensive and defensive players, neither of whom may survive a violent confrontation. Further, college players wear metal spikes, and these can cause calamitous injuries. Plastic spikes can do their share of damage, too.

There is plenty of room for injury when fielders are forced to move into the path of a runner when the ball takes them in that direction. These situations are part of the game and, although unfortunate, they will occur. Why on earth would we want to multiply the dangerous situations by intentional, illegal defensive positioning?

When asked how their seasons went, coaches often reply, "We had a lot of injuries." No more need be said, for it is implied in the statement that the season did not go well.

Although it is disheartening to lose key players at any level, college games are very aggressively played, and coaches are especially devastated by key injuries. Lots of hard work went into recruiting impact players who occupy the skill positions on the field. Such players are integral to a successful season. While in season, each is exposed to injury on a daily basis. Off-season has its share of injury mischief, too, for we often find our kids tripping over a foul line or slipping on a banana peel. Then, why do we add to problems by placing our kids in harm's way? It is truly a mystery.

Chapter 8
AGRESSIVE BASE RUNNERS
WARM MY HEART

Getting to first base is only part of the struggle in the game of softball, although it sometimes seems impossible, given some of the fine pitchers and defenses we face. So, once there it would seem fitting that we take advantage of the situation and do everything possible to advance, hopefully to our final goal, home. Keep in mind that when the pitchers are "on" the nitty-gritty gets tough to chew.

Normal methods to advance our runners beyond first base are numerous and are fundamentally sound for the most part. All coaches are aware of the blueprints, although some, it would seem, forget the plans from time to time.

Once at first, our leadoff is a critical factor in whether or not we advance. Coaches teach various methods to take a lead-off, but whatever is used must be explosive and on balance. When not stealing, runners must be in a position which will allow them to return to the base safely to avoid the cannon-like pickoff some catchers possess. Yes, runners can be aggressive even when not stealing. A good runner can befuddle a defense, making them think she is going on each pitch. That, of course, sets up the real steal, or hit and run as the "cry wolf" syndrome takes effect.

When not stealing, runners should lead off behind the baseline by as much as three feet. This increases the distance to second a bit, but there are a couple of unmistakable advantages involved.

A lead behind the baseline automatically establishes a turn around second base. This avoids a kick out at second or a large turn into left field, both of which lengthen the time to third. Secondly, runners have better access to the bag when going back to the base on a pick off attempt, as they are able to go for the rear of the base, thus preventing the first baseman from blocking their access and making a tag more difficult.

In connection with all leads, the dive must be taught. Now, I mean dive, not the normal crash associated with most returns to a base. This involves staying low to the ground, cushioning the fall with the left hand by keeping the arm and wrist bent, and pushing the body along the ground. The right hand is used to reach for the base, while the helmeted head turns to right field. This head turn will allow runners to search for errant throws into the outfield providing potential for advancement, and will, more importantly, protect the runner from a serious bonk on the noggin.

Now, runners, and fielders too, have a tendency to raise their bodies up when beginning to run. This, of course, slows them down. Remember, that each one tenth of a second saved is two feet. Rising up when one begins to run will have a definite price. So runners need to stay low.

Stealing is becoming a lost art these days, particularly with the advent of more adept catchers and catching techniques. This strategy, or rather the lack thereof, is surprising in view of the tendency of coaches to look for speedy runners. I wonder at the wisdom of gaining speed if one does not use it. Are the catchers that good? Hmmm?

So do successful runners "cheat" when leaving a base? That is, do they leave the base illegally before the ball is released by the pitcher? Many do, it would seem, and umpires tend to give the runners a great deal of leeway here. I have viewed videos in slow motion of some runners who appear to be leaving "early." Sur-

---

SMITTY SAYS:

A word of caution. Coaches should not use the word "no" where there is passed ball or wild pitch and they want the runner to say on third. It sounds too much like "go," and we wouldn't want to confuse the issue. Use "stay," instead. Anyway, if you want your runners to be aggressive, let them make the decision to go or stay. It is the same with fly balls. Smitty will guarantee more runs if you let the runners decide. Don't agree do you, coach? Guess you've never been wrong about sending a runner, eh?

prisingly, they often appear to be early because they are in motion, but the camera shows clearly that most are exactly on time.

Umpires have the most difficulty with the "rocking" start from bases. Thus players and coaches must be alert for those who call runners out because they see movement and not because the runners are leaving early. This puts a definite damper on steals and squeeze plays.

Okay, we have reached second base, now what? We need the same aggressive leads here. However, the runner must be even more explosive and assertive, daring the adventuresome catcher to throw. Pickoff attempts at second are rarely successful, offer a great opportunity for delayed steals, and are not much of a concern for alert runners. Such leads from second enhance our chances for successful scores, and we should not be that fretful about the pickoff. We are, of course, vulnerable to being doubled off should a line drive be hit, but the venturesome oft encounter woes when venturing. So we coaches should not be too hard on our players when such adversities occur, for they are to be expected with an aggressive offense.

When using aggressive leads, second base runners are almost certainly committed to third on a ball hit anywhere on the ground. Although this will lead to outs on occasion, the pugnacity of runners will more times than not create defensive confusion. A shot to a shortstop sometimes turns into trepidation as a runner whizzes by on her way to third. The ensuing panic often creates a hurried, open-shouldered, and routinely errant, throw to third.

On to third and then to home. Now we must be very careful about the cannons of the good catchers. Too much aggressiveness in leading off can create horrifying situations. The unwary coming off the base in an unbalanced fashion, or returning in a ho-hum manner, risks disaster. Get off the base aggressively, but return just as aggressively.

Make certain runners lead off in foul territory and return to the bag in fair. Runners are simply not taught to do this, but it is most important. Not much is worse than being hit by a worm burner or blue darter, unless it is getting whacked in fair territory. The former causes body pain, but the latter additionally causes embarrassment and unhappy coaches. Returning to the base in fair territory avoids problems, messes up the catcher's target, the fielder's line of sight to the ball, and offers a substantially better method of getting back safely.

You might want to introduce a "contact offense." This means runners go on contact, no matter what. If the ball is up, they try to get back, but otherwise they take off when the ball is hit. Yes, you do it even if the runner is on third and the third baseman gets the ball. By the time the fielder "looks the runner back," she is zipping by on her way home. Excited fielders often throw in a hurry and bad throws frequently result. Even if the throw is good and the runner is caught, the batter-runner should be merrily on her way to second, or possibly, third base.

Ah, aggressiveness. How it warms the heart of the offensive-minded coach and leads to run production. Oh, the fun that awaits teams which have the pugnacity to be fearless on the base paths. It leads to home sweet home...the place to be.

Part Three:
TAKE TO THE FIELD

Chapter 9
WON'T SOMEONE PLEASE
CATCH THE BALL?

Watching games and participating in camps are favorite pastimes of mine. One sees all kinds of ways to do things on these occasions. I analyze and theorize about what I have seen, and then I discuss my conclusions with other coaches; yes, and even with players. If I get enough agreement, and even if I don't, I gather that my assumptions are correct and put them into operation on my team. Let's address one of these conclusions emanating from this process.

The typical game is often won or lost as a result of how things are done, or not done. Rather obvious, no? But, guess what? Coaches are loath to address their players' misfeasance, malfeasance, or even their "feasances."

For example, the simple act of catching a ball incorrectly has resulted in the loss of countless ball games and has to rate as one of the colossal reasons teams have problems winning. Yet, very limited time, if any, is spent on this most important aspect of the game. Flagrant fundamental violations occur and go seemingly unnoticed. There is seldom an effort to determine why a ball was dropped. And I am referring not only to the younger set. These violations occur at the very highest levels of softball. Let's examine the problem.

Anyone (well, almost anyone) can catch a good throw, but a person in the act of catching a ball thrown by another person should be prepared for a bad throw, not a good one. This means the receiver must have a balanced stance, with bent knees, and both hands out providing a target. Since the ball may go in any direction, the receiver must be prepared to move to catch it.

"Elementary, my dear Watson!" exclaimed Sherlock Holmes. But, take the time to watch your team warm up. Make notes, because, on average, you will see the following: receivers with feet close together, which fosters poor balance and subsequent poor movement; no movement to get in front of the ball; "brick hands," that is poor "give" as they receive the ball; poor transfer of the ball from the glove to the throwing hand; and general sloppy and lazy workouts. It is Smitty's Law that in these cases, your players are practicing errors.

If you can, videotape the warm-up and show it to your players. Ask their opinion about their catching techniques. Point out the weaknesses in slow motion. See if they are interested in correcting the faults or whether they would rather continue their slipshod methods. I'd wager that they will be surprised at their sloppiness and want to improve.

The catching of a thrown ball is one thing. A "routine" fly ball is another. Best you forget the word "routine." Gordie Gillespie, the great baseball coach at the College of St. Francis, once said (actually he said it many times), "There is no such thing as a routine catch. You should treat every one as if the World Series depended upon it, because it does." He, of course, was and is right.

Take the time to watch your players during fly ball practice. Note the lazy approaches to the ball, the poor movement of the feet, the casual manner in which the ball is caught and then thrown, and the failure to drop step. These are critical matters and must be addressed if your team is to be successful.

The fly ball is a gift from the hitter. It is what I call a "thank you" ball. It is an out. We must take advantage of the generosity of the offense and work hard to receive the booty so graciously offered.

While on the subject of catching flies, it is duly noted that catches should be two-handed if possible. But most fly balls are hit away from the fielders, not directly in their laps. Sometimes, they must dive to make a catch. So it becomes incumbent upon the fielders to learn to run with their gloves in and extend, one handed, to the ball. Why use only one hand to catch a ball when we have been taught to use two ever since we can remember? Well, there's better balance and a greater reach resulting in more catches.

The blasphemy continues. Infielders, including first basemen, will also benefit from the one-handed catch. Not only do they have better reach, but they can leap higher one-handed than were they to do it with two.

SMITTY SAYS:

Improvement requires that correct methods be taught and then diligently practiced under the watchful eyes of coaches. These same coaches must be intolerant of sloppy performance on the practice field. Care of equipment is just as important and must be emphasized. It is a fundamental truth that a team will play in the same manner in which it has practiced.

More caught balls will contribute to the well-being of your record and, of course, your general coaching disposition. Will those dispositions take an adverse turn should the ball be dropped by a one-handed attempt? Sure, but it's temporary, and their mettle will improve on average if the technique is routinely used.

Another ingredient that affects catching a ball has to do with glove conditioning. If a glove is broken in correctly, wiped off after each use, and appropriately oiled, it will provide remarkable service for many years. The breaking-in process involves molding the glove into a basket shape with the hands, again and again, over a long period of time. In between innings, gloves should be placed down correctly. That involves putting the glove pocket side down and resting on the fingers of the glove, rather than indiscriminately tossing to on the ground as most players do. When the game is over, the glove should be cleaned and oiled. Then the player should put a ball in it, tie it up with a belt, and put it in her bag.

Note that glove oil tends to rot leather. A little old shoemaker once told me that the best product to put on the outside and inside of a glove is a product that shall remain nameless, but it is one that mothers put on their hands to soften them. After all, gloves are made out of skin, so why not use the same thing?

I guarantee 10 percent fewer errors if players will take care of their gloves. How outrageously simple!

And remember, there are many elements of the game of softball. Catching the ball is just one of them.

Chapter 10
DEFENSIVE STUFF

So, now you've come to midseason and trouble looms concerning the win column. How come? Can't hit? Can't field. "Giving" games away, eh coach? Well, maybe it's time to look at our defensive checklist, a task that should have been given more attention during preseason workouts. But it's not too late as long as we are able to recognize a boiling pot and the meaning of the opponents words when they say, "Put a fork in them. They're done!"

"Hey," says you. "We're hittin' the livin' begeezers out of the ball! No problem there. Pitchin' seems OK. We're losin' it somewhere else."

In the field?

"Yeah! We keep makin' those dumb mistakes. If it ain't mental errors, it's throwin' or catchin' the stupid ball. And we always seem to do it at the wrong time. Things will be goin' great, but then we blow it with a dumb play. Lousy fielding!"

Let's separate mental and physical errors. Sometimes they are one and the same, but throwing to the wrong base, forgetting the outs, not backing up a base, etc., are purely mental. The causes for mental errors are myriad. So much so that one cannot really discuss them and come to any sort of conclusion. There are a few, however, that we should try to control so that it does not look like our players are making deliberate attempts to throw games for the gamblers.

Contributors to the poor mental awareness include, but are not limited to: lousy eating habits, late hours, failure of the coach to prepare the team, being on the road, lack of hustle, lack of caring, lack of practice, sloppy practice, sloppy uniforms, sloppy attitude, and the like.

What about the actual fielding part? Note that pitching and hitting clinics usually have excellent attendance. But, put on a fielding camp and the joint will be deserted. Seems that players, coaches,

---

SMITTY SAYS:

Coaches must understand how to get the information they have acquired across to the kids with whom they are working. We in the trade call it teaching. Sometimes teaching is a whole lot tougher than one might think. It requires patience, understanding, and, above all, communication.

---

and parents relegate the fine art of fielding to a low station in life. However, it is Smitty's law that fielding clinics should be routinely attended by all, since a ball that is properly fielded normally will impact a record more favorably than one that is not.

Let's look at a few of the little devilish items that should command our attention, but often do not.

Bad Throws:
- Are the players gripping the ball across the seams?
- Are they throwing over the top, using the non-throwing side to gain power?
- Are they throwing open-shouldered rather than keeping the front side closed?
- Do they bring their throwing-side hip through as they throw?
- Do they throw into a slightly bent front leg or do they block their hips by throwing into a stiff front leg?
- Do they take a big stride and launch the ball into outer space?
- Do they use the crow hop in the outfield? Or better stated, do they use it properly by stepping forward with their back foot?
- Do they try to overpower the throw, especially when near their target, rather than using a run-through, soft toss, or a backhand flip?
- Does the shortstop "load up" properly when going into the hole between short and third base?
- Do the players push the ball as they throw, or otherwise

bend their throwing hand in weird contortions behind their heads?

Well, if you have problems with the above, you certainly do have problems. If throws are off target and going all over the place, it is suggested that you look at the above checklist, which is by no means all-inclusive. If you don't know how to correct the problems, find someone who can, or else the season will only get longer for you.

Are there problems with catching the ball? Ask yourself the following questions:

- Are your players looking the ball into their gloves?
- Do they try to always catch the ball in the web of the glove so as not to hurt their hands, rather than in the pocket where the ball is meant to be caught?
- Do they try to throw the ball before they receive it?
- Are their arms slightly bent when catching or do they extend them fully, thus eliminating any hope of having soft hands?
- Are they prepared for a bad throw, realizing that anyone can catch a good one?
- Are their legs bent when receiving the ball and are their hands ready for a two-handed catch wherever possible?
- Are they running hard on difficult catches with their gloves in until the very last moment when they should extend for the ball?

Well, if you are having problems with the above, you certainly do have problems. Catching the ball seems to be a lost art in some games. There has been many a college game where supposedly superior athletes have failed to make what is considered to be a routine catch. Remember, there is no such thing as a routine catch, by the way.

There are many other particulars that cause defensive faults. Not every coach is totally knowledgeable about all matters pertaining to such things. What's more, knowledge is not the only thing required. Clearly, defense is not the sum total of that which is required to gain victory. Without it, opponents' offenses will never be frustrated...only nurtured.

Chapter 11
COMING UP SHORT

She did what?

"Well," says MacCoachski. "We were up 2-1 in the bottom of the seventh, and they had runners on second and third. There was a routine, bouncing ball, and the shortstop booted it. When she finally picked it up, she threw the ball into the ground, bouncing it past the first baseman. We lost the big game."

Zounds! Did she do it on purpose? Was she possessed? Did the Mafia pay her off?

"Well, I don't think it was any of the above. These things keep happening, day in and day out. I simply don't know why."

I do.

"You Do? Pray, tell! How, why, and what!"

Posturing in my "know-it-all" suit, I analyzed the apparent mystery.

Other than the often overlooked factor that her glove was probably too big, I bet your shortstop (along with many of your other players) tends to flip the ball from the glove to the throwing hand as she prepares to throw.

"What?"

Yes, most players do this. Coaches must be very observant to see this little gem. Instead of catching a ball, covering it with the throwing hand, and bringing the glove and the ball back into a throwing position, players often flip the ball from the glove to the throwing hand. This can be seen while kids are warming up. It causes them to have a poor grip on the ball or to drop it from time to time, maybe even cause a late throw from fielders, including catchers on steal attempts. It's Smitty's law that players who flip the ball from their gloves to their hands are practicing errors.

Next problem concerns the throw itself. Did your shortstop throw against her body?

"What?" Here coach looked perplexed.

Yes, did she throw into a stiff front leg preventing her follow-through? Balls are often launched into outer space by this little maneuver. Coaches should watch to see if players are correctly bending their front knee and following through with their shoulder and hip, allowing for a correct, low throw. A little observation during practices might make this unmistakably clear and prevent later problems.

Of course, one apparent problem is often created by another.

"What," he asks, scratching his chin.

You see, when a player has a long stride, she comes down on her heel. This not only jars her body, but also prevents a follow-through and causes her to throw high. Typically, this is the reason there are overthrows.

"Well, Mr. All-the-Answers, she didn't throw toward Mars like you said. She threw the ball into the dirt!"

That's correct, but did you watch her just before the count-down launch?

"What?"

Yes, when preparing to throw, many players bend their throwing arm behind their heads, causing their wrists to turn in grotesque ways, generally toward the outfield. Coach, you should watch to see that the wrist comes straight back as the body turns. Further, the throwing arm should be a nice "L" shape as it proceeds toward the rear, rather than in some convoluted condition behind the body. Indeed, these contortions tend to cause throws to go hippity-hoppity into the ground.

"Yeah! And then the first baseman has a heck of a problem. Can't put any blame on her."

So you believe her function is to catch only good throws?

SMITTY SAYS:

Often in pregame, you can't take to the infield, but you can have the line drills. Challenge your players in these drills by hitting balls right, left, soft, and hard. The players enjoy it, and it really helps in the game.

"What?" Beads of perspiration began dripping off his forehead.

For your information, a first baseman's function is to try and catch all throws, not just the good ones. If that is not possible, at least she must knock them down or otherwise stop them. She must be a veritable contortionist who jumps, dives, and scrambles to stop balls from getting by her.

It would be wise for all those receiving throws to make a negative assumption before a throw is actually made. Players must think, "My teammate is going to make an error. She is going to throw the ball away. I must be prepared to catch it."

Just as a great defense can keep a pitcher's ERA low, a great first baseman can keep the fielding averages of the other fielders very high.

But, back to the shortstop. How about the practices? How many balls have you hit to her left? To her right? Softly, so she must charge the ball? Hit any fly balls to your infielders, coach?

"Of course, I've challenged my players. I've hit lots of grounders."

Come on now, coach, have you really challenged them by giving them the most difficult plays you can imagine, or have you hit candy hops, buddy-buddy grounders, and lazy fly balls? Players have to work! They must be challenged and put to the test. Practice is where it's done. Coaching clinics and good fundamental books are where it's learned. You must learn and then teach. Once your players have learned from you, the bad throws will be few, and those that are will be snagged by your first baseman.

Chapter 12
HAND 'N GLOVE

Don't suppose you have ever seen a fielder make a clean pickup on a ground ball and then as she prepares her footwork to throw, everything suddenly goes out of sync? Sure, you have. She gropes for the ball in her glove. She can't find it in the huge cowhide covering her catching hand. Then she does find it, but horrors! She gets a lousy grip, and either throws it away or the runner is safe due to the lull in the fielding action.

The huge gloves kids wear today are more of a hindrance than a benefit. Solution: A smaller glove; one that the player can feel the ball in; one that is flexible; and one that is a bit lighter than the monster most players use. A smaller, lighter glove means quickness....quicker left, forward, and backward; well just plain quicker.

Faster hands are crucial, so that a 60 mph grounder can be frustrated on its intended nomadic journey to the outfield. Quickness is the key.

But with old Glovius Gigantius, delight will prevail on your opponent's bench as their teammates romp about the bases. The leather monster is also quite adept at hiding a ball and frustrating a fielder's attempt to retrieve it for a play. Watch sometime as fielders grope in their gloves for the ball. Can't find it, eh? Oh, well, didn't want to win this one anyway.

SMITTY SAYS:

Larger gloves give younger players a false sense of security by making them believe they'll be able to catch more balls. Erroneous thinking. Smitty suggests that middle infielders and third basemen get smaller gloves. They will be quicker and better fielders. Count on it!

Some agree that a smaller glove is good in the infield, but what about pitchers, first basemen, catchers, and outfielders? Wouldn't a big glove be better for them? Maybe so, if you decide that quickness is not a requisite for them. But this is an individual decision, and I will not win this one.

Speaking of gloves, how come manufacturers create gloves that a vise in a woodworking shop could not squeeze shut over a ball? The leather is hard, inflexible, and takes a lifetime to break in. In the meantime, the leather rots, the lacing breaks and the pocket develops holes. Built in obsolescence?

I have a beauty of a glove, made more than a few moons ago. It is still "operational." It is flexible and soft. But a salesman at a clinic I attended did not care for it. He brought out one of his iron-age creations for comparison. He used injurious words whilst touching and wearing my beauty. I snatched it away and pointed out that my glove has lasted lo these many years, and there was one great difference between my belle and his despicable leather abomination.

"Oh, yeah? And what would that be?" he delicately inquired.

My glove does not make errors!!! I kid you not.

Chapter 13
A SAGA OF THE THREE WAIFS OF SOFTBALL

The Wicked Witch of the East made a proclamation sometime prior to about 1985. She ordained that fastpitch softball pitchers shall prevail by adroitly whizzing the ball to the plate at various speeds up to 70 mph. Batters reluctantly submitted and batting averages became unwell. She directed that the potentates of softball were to be the pitchers. Pretenders to the throne included catchers and shortstops. Other fielders were to occupy stations quite below these positions, but were to retain a trifle of importance. Last in succession were the lowly outfielders, and last in that group was the wretched and unworthy right fielders.

But lo! The knighted ones (coaches) began to attend clinics and learn. More knowledgeable teachers came across the moat and hitting prospered. Even though pitchers in general upped their speed and became better at their trade, the hitters became even more adroit and began making solid contact with pitches that theretofore eluded their bats.

The wretched outfielders became more wretched as ball after ball eluded them and batting averages began to soar. Worse yet, the softball gurus ordained that the college pitching distance should be moved to 43 feet. Although this did not affect younger outfielders, the die was cast unless something could save the outfielders from their destiny.

But lo, again. The knights forgot about the waifs of the outfield. They did not prosper as did pitchers and hitters. Most clinicians routinely ignored outfield play. Even when the topic was on the agenda, rooms emptied quickly as coaches searched for more captivating subjects such as pitching and hitting.

Recently, there has been some thought given to outfield play at clinics, and gradually coaches are beginning to comprehend that this aspect of the game is routinely horrendous and is responsible for an untold number of losses. So, what can be done?

SMITTY SAYS:

Get some whiffle balls and wait for a sunny day. Place your fielders so that they are looking into the sun. Teach your kids to cover the sun with their glove or their free hand, which-ever you prefer. Then toss the balls so that they must catch them while fighting off the sun's rays. Do this on several occasions.

Start by making a few proclamations of your own, namely: the outfield is just as important as any other position; right field is equally important; the outfield is the last line of defense; the out-field will have equal practice time; it will not be ignored by the coaches; good outfield play will help win games just as poor play will lose them; and the outfield must limit damage by stopping hit balls as soon as possible.

The requirements for outfielders are speed afoot, a good arm, and a belief in the importance of their position. We coaches are not always blessed with the first two criteria, but with training in proper techniques, practice, and some innovative ideas, we can sometimes cover up weaknesses. For example, if we have slow outfielders, we can increase their ability to get a jump on the ball by good footwork. If arms are weak, we can make better use of our relays.

Several items concerning outfield techniques merit attention. Outfielders must:

1. Learn the drop step.
2. Use visualization to focus on the hitting zone as the ball is pitched.
3. Stay low when taking the first steps to the ball.
4. Learn to run with their gloves in, extending only at the last possible moment.
5. Pump their arms as they run.
6. Learn to violently explode in the direction that will allow them to catch or stop the ball.
7. Learn to communicate to avoid collisions.

8. Work hard on relays.
9. Learn to grip the ball across the seams to enhance proper ball rotation.
10. Practice the long throw, stretching the arm, back, and leg muscles.
11. Practice catching all kinds of fly balls.
12. Round off fly balls and grounders.
13. Lean to handle obstacles — the wind, sun, rain, wet ground, hard ground, bumpy ground, cold weather, hot weather, rude spectators.
14. Et cetera. (hate to end on 13).

The trouble with having a good pitcher is that outfielders get little game practice. So, boredom sets in and daydreaming decides to overcome reality. This condition is especially prevalent with younger kids who see precious few balls hit their way.

Unless outfielders are well coached, games can get pretty gruesome. Suddenly…well, you guessed it. A ball rockets by the outfielders, and they lose precious steps whilst exiting their repose. This always happens at the worst possible time in a game. What could have been a routine catch, has become a horror with the ball rolling on its merry way to the fence. Oh, well, such circumstances give rise to relay practice, so all is not lost.

Clearly there is more to the outfield than hitting a few fly balls in practice. There is far more to it than deciding where to hide your poorest player and where to play your other misfits.

If you want to be included in our saga, you may apply merely by ignoring your three waifs. It is incumbent upon you to work hard on outfield techniques so that your charges will progress from waifdom to stardom, providing you with some memorable moments. It is Smitty's law that great plays are not accidents, since they are the result of properly trained athletes executing fundamentals properly.

Part Four:
TO BE A PITCHER

Chapter 14
PATIENCE, PATIENCE, AND MORE PATIENCE

When learning any task, including softball basics, patience is more than virtue. It is mandatory. Let us demonstrate. We will take the fine art of pitching as our example, although the following also applies to all the other softball skills as well.

By way of background, we must examine certain athletic absolutes. Winning is all-important. To fail is abominable, disgusting, and loathsome. Losers are losers. Failure is to be scorned, detested, and avoided at all costs. Ha!

The "must win" and "must not lose" syndromes are rampant in today's athletic world and will someday spell the doom of athletics as we know them. But, that is a subject for another day. Suffice it to say that our syndromes saturate athletic attitudes, including those of parents.

With this in mind, Mr. (or Mrs. or Ms.) Papa brings his nine-year-old daughter, Sibling, quaintly nicknamed Sib, to pitching camp. She is going out for the hometown team and needs to learn how to toss the old pill. She has been "pitching" for awhile, but not too well, to say the least.

Sib takes the instruction, leaves, but typically returns to the pitching coach because, as Mr. Papa says, "She isn't fast enough and can't throw strikes!"

More lessons ensue, but improvement doesn't. Mr. Papa is discouraged and yells at Sib, but Sib doesn't respond except to secretly cry. Mr. Papa wants instant, yes, instant improvement and is not getting his money's worth.

Is it to be? Can Sib, at the ripe old age of nine, 12, or even in advanced teen years, achieve that peculiarity which Mr. Papa has entrusted to the venerable pitching coach? That is, instant success!

But what is success to Mr. Papa? Success is accomplishing the absolutes already mentioned. She must throw strikes, with speed, and win the game. Nothing else matters. If you have ever given pitching lessons, you will understand this scenario. It is often re-peated and will ever endure. We cannot even hope to eliminate the syndromes. But in the meantime…

The pitching coach tells Mr. Papa that this will take time. Sib will not master the techniques overnight. Indeed, it may take months or years before she will be a true pitcher. She needs hours and hours of practice, coupled with expert instruction on the finer points of pitching. It will take conditioning, physical growth, prac-tice, and time. In the end, if Sib works hard and has the ability, she should become a decent pitcher.

"Decent! Decent, you say? Why, my daughter must be the best. She will command the respect of all in high school and will be courted by all the college coaches. Why, she will be able to attend any Division I school she likes, at no cost. She will get a full ride!" Of this, Mr. Papa is certain.

The kindhearted pitching coach listens, nodding in mocked agreement, but eventually tries to rebut Mr. Papa's contentions in a soothing and simple way. Coach will say that to become a great pitcher, Sib must suffer through many, many bad games. She must weather the storm, fight her way through, and if she has the de-termination to overcome and work hard, she will probably prevail in the end. All great pitchers have gone through this stage. None was ever an instant success.

Mr. Papa is disillusioned with the pitching coach. He cannot understand the coach's words, cautions, and sentiments. He may nod his head in pretended agreement, but he either does not hear what is said or chooses to ignore it.

Meanwhile, Mr. Papa talks to others and becomes a self-ap-pointed expert in the art of pitching. He ain't stupid, however, and realizes he doesn't know it all, even though he tries to make everyone think he does. So he takes Sib to another pitching guru.

The new coach observes, makes some changes, and one out of 10 pitches looks relatively good. At these junctures of apparent success, the new coach yells, "Way to go. See, when you do it right, you get good pitches."

Now, by way of definition, a good pitch is one that is reason-ably fast and goes directly into the strike zone. It matters not that the pitch would be in a good hitter's "wheelhouse" and would be

> ## SMITTY SAYS:
>
> *Players, parents, and coaches must all possess vast amounts of patience, not only for each other but for the ever-surprising process of the game. Patience is the true absolute and will assist in achieving your goals.*

propelled into orbit in a real game. What is important is that the pitch looked fast and was a strike!

Progress, at last. Now to the game.

But, lo! Mr. Papa returns and tells the new coach that not only was the control lousy, but every strike was hit so hard his daughter needed a suit of armor. Please fix it.

Back to the drawing board. Mr. Papa, however, does not like the drawings. So there is more yelling, or quiet criticism, each having much the same result on Sib's attitude as she becomes more and more frustrated. Onward to the yellow pages for another coach.

If Sib doesn't quit the game, or at least pitching, she will continue reluctantly or defiantly. She may become a decent pitcher, depending upon her will and ability. Coupled with proper coaching, she may even become great. However, the vast majority cross over the pitching rubber to the other perils of life which await them. The dream of greatness on the mound becomes a nightmare.

The dream, of course, is to pitch for a top college softball team in the NCAA. Ah, but dreams are so fragile, riddled with such flimsy and brittle hopes. Most pitching dreams end in a puff of smoke at some point in any career where instant success is expected and even demanded.

Hence, coaches, here's some advice to share with the aspiring softballer. Feel free to use my words verbatim: If you desire to succeed at pitching, you absolutely must do certain things. Find a good pitching coach, a venture that is fraught with danger because of the scarcity of good ones and the abundance of impostors. Give the coach a chance, and then practice what is taught. Remember that every great pitcher has gone through exactly the same frustrations and difficulties that you will experience. Patience on your part is essential.

Hence, also, here's some advice to share with the parent(s) of the aspiring softballer. Let those who know do the coaching. Allow the coaches to do their jobs. Stay out of your daughter's face. Encourage her, but be realistic too. Help her through her times of frustration. She must not be babied, but she needs encouragement. Never undercut her accomplishments, but never flaunt or exaggerate her capabilities either. Just let her do her thing and be supportive. Above all, have patience.

Chapter 15
THE FIFTH INFIELDER

Many of the great sages throughout time used parables to get their point across. Following in the footsteps of the masters, I have decided to do the same regarding a matter of great importance -- the fifth infielder. Pay close attention.

So, little pitcher, how did practice go?

"Well, pretty good," says Felicia Flameshooter. "I threw 150 pitches today, plus my warm-ups."

Cool, but what else?

"Nothing. Oh, if you mean stretching, I did that and ran some before I pitched."

No fielding practice?

"No, why?" she asks.

Well, let me count the "whys." Please note that there are some very good fielding pitchers, but past observations have indicated that the majority of hurlers are "pitch oriented." That is, once they throw the ball in the direction of the plate, they figure their business is completed until they have to throw the ball again. Even when balls are hit well past their position, pitchers love to watch the outcome from their lofty bivouacs near the mound. They regularly fail to back up plays during the ensuing action, and they pretty much stand around complaining that the coach or the catcher called the wrong pitch.

Felicia, you don't want to always have the coach telling you what to do and where to go after a ball is hit, do you? It is understandable if you are "game dense" (clueless as to what to do), but most pitchers are reasonably intelligent about the game and can be trained in the fine art of doing the right thing when a ball is hit.

Such softball pitching delinquencies, however, pale in comparison to others. These concern a failure to field balls hit up the middle; poor throws by pitchers to a base, usually first; errant throws to home plate on squeeze plays; and covering the plate on pitches that get by the catcher.

"But Smitty," protests Felicia, "My dad hits me grounders at practice."

Yeah, but how often and how hard? You get candy hops hit right at you, and you know they are coming so that you are already in a fielding position. How about getting some line drives and hard hit balls a split second after you have pitched a ball. Yes, you can pitch to a catcher standing beside a coach and have the coach hit a ball at you about the time the pitch reaches the catcher. These should simulate game conditions and should be hit to your right and left, at varying speeds. This should be done at every practice.

Also, little pitcher, you might try getting your rear end down to field the grounders, rather than bending at the waist. Yeah, try groveling for the ball like the rest of the infield. It's okay to get your uniform dirty, you know.

Tell your coach to throw whiffle balls back at you. You can use your full motion, and coach can whip the ball back from about ten feet. These should be high, low, and like a line drive. Works great.

"Well, okay, but I've got a really good arm!"

Yes, you do. It's so fine that when throwing to first base, the right fielder has fun running after the ball. Have you noticed the throws are all high? The first baseman has little chance to catch the ball. It would be better to roll the ball on the ground than to fling it into orbit .

"You're kidding, Smitty! You don't really want me to roll the ball, do you?"

No, but if you did roll it, the person at first would at least have a chance to catch it. Remember, that when you throw high it is because you are overthrowing, overstriding and/or standing straight up after you field a ball, and then you launch it by throwing against your body.

On those occasions when you do throw it in the dirt, it is usually because you have no confidence in the throw and take too much off. You accomplish this by taking your throwing arm way back, and then you try to slow down the forward movement of your arm as you throw the ball.

All this may be hard for you to visualize, but you must make every effort to get your throws to your target. You can start by working on every overhand throw you make as you warm up. Look for a target each time and then try to hit it. Maybe, with some practice, your basemen will be able to use their gloves instead of their legs.

"Yes, but what's this about squeeze bunts? I rarely ever see one."

You are right. There aren't many such situations at your age and level of play, and those that occur involve basically slow and unskilled runners. But what about the future when you go up in level, and when the opponents realize you can't field a bunt? It won't take them long, you know.

Basically, you do the same thing on bunts that you do on other plays. You get to the ball, field it, stand up, and then throw. You should learn to field by staying low and then make a low, "soft" throw to the catcher by using an underhand toss or backhand flip. The key is to stay low as you field and then make the throw, staying low. If you stand up as you field the ball, you will lose time and the ball may be overthrown.

You should also work hard on the "run through" throw or toss. Simply put, you charge the ball, field it and then flip it to your target, all on the run. Takes practice, but it makes for a nice, soft throw that the catcher can easily handle, even if it's off target.

"Yes, but..."

Now, don't tell me how good you are at covering the plate. The way you are doing it will get you a nice trip to the emergency room. It is far better to have no outs than an injured pitcher. Good pitchers are tough to replace.

In general, you loaf getting to the plate. When there is a runner on third, you must soothsay that every pitch will be wild. You should be prepared to sprint for the plate immediately, not tomorrow. Go as fast as you can, and then get your body under control as you reach the plate. Keep your feet to the inside of the baseline,

SMITTY SAYS:

Coach, how about hitting some hot grounders at your pitchers once in a while?

giving the runner the back part of the plate. Bend your knees, get your rear end down, and prepare for a bad throw from the catcher. Make sure you catch it one-handed and then make the tag in a sweeping motion, after which you must immediately get your feet out of the way by moving to the inside of the diamond. Be prepared at this point to throw to another base if there are other runners meandering about.

"Sounds too complicated for me."

Felicia, it isn't. It's basic stuff. If you do not field your position, there is a monstrous hole up the middle. This is where good batters are trained to hit. If you aren't there, no one else will be and woe to your ERA. Yes, you are not only a pitcher, but an infielder, as well. In fact, you are the fifth infielder.

Chapter 16
SPEED IS NICE, BUT VARIETY IS...

"I don't understand it!"

I was taken aback. Don't understand what, Sally Flamethrower?

"Well, for years I heaved my fastball right by all the hitters, and now it seems all my outfielders are getting lots of exercise, and my ERA...oh, woe, my ERA is exhibiting signs of hypertension and is headed off the charts. Not only that, but my ears have been buzzed by blue darters, and I hopscotched over a few hot ones up the middle. I fear an involuntary appendectomy at any moment. I'm simply mortified, not to mention my chagrin at a probable deportation to the bullpen."

Let's look at human nature a moment. The "I wanna throw fast" syndrome usually infects its host sometime around the time a pitcher, a parent, or a coach gets the notion that she has a "good wrist." Speed becomes the total focus, and the recipe for disaster begins to fester.

Yes, it is the normal state of affairs for young pitchers to work hard to develop speed. The watchwords are: "Speed first; control will follow."

Perhaps true, perhaps not. It seems clear that technique comes into play here somewhere. Maybe with good form and fundamentals, speed and control will develop simultaneously.

As they progress along the ranks of development, young pitchers will say, "I'm not throwing fast enough!"

With this in mind, particularly if a radar gun is present, the pitching neophytes will give it their all and, in the process, put one or more critical mistakes into their deliveries. Their timing will go haywire and when that happens, all sorts of miserable things manifest themselves. The result is that speed will go down, not up.

Now, let's crawl into the mind of a batter. She also deals with timing, although she is seldom conscious of the fact. If you throw enough fastballs at her, she will learn to hit them. Likewise, should you throw nothing but change-ups, she will do the same. If you alternate the two, she will begin to have problems. These problems are magnified if you really mix them up.

If you add a third pitch, such as a drop, a riser, or a knuckleball, the hitter's timing is baffled even more. Complications become more complicated when pitches are coupled with location.

These ideas seem to be fundamental, do they not? Yet, pitchers, parents, and coaches will forever be possessed by the demon known as speed.

Well, I have a law that says if one relies on speed alone, there better be a very good outfield available, and one which is very conditioned in the art of relays. As one advances in the levels of softball, this becomes more and more apparent.

The speed syndrome appears to have evolved from several years ago when pitchers were more than able to use velocity to dominate hitters. It is true today, as well, in the lower levels of softball where kids have not developed hitting skills.

But, lo! Hitters have teachers too, and they have begun to learn. Coaches have attended clinics, talked about the art of hitting, and have learned the mystery of teaching such things to their charges. The result is that hitters have learned to hit. Amazing!

So what can be done to confound the emergence of hitting proficiency?

Not too many moons ago, a pitcher won the a national championship with what some call the "backhand change." Her fastball could not break a pane of glass, so she used it as a "change," keeping it all the while out of the strike zone. No one hit her. No one.

How come the hitters had so much trouble? Well, it had to do with timing. If a batter's timing is thrown off, she becomes a piece of cake, or, rather, an out. Hitters at the aforementioned championship kept expecting a fastball, but got none in the zone.

Today, pitchers can be seen throwing excellent off-speed pitches. They are very effective. But then suddenly, the speed syndrome strikes, and they feel they must throw it by the hitter.

Wham! The outfielders are on the move again. Yes, hitters are aware of the "fastball syndrome." They know pitchers love to strike them out. They know they will be challenged. Consequently, they sit back and wait on the pumpkins to arrive.

SMITTY SAYS:

So, coach, know that speed is nice, but variety is the oregano and basil of pitching. It will, in most cases, make a very delicious duck soup out of the most powerful of sluggers.

"So, Mr. Knowitallski, won't hitters suspect a change of speed if you throw the pitch often? Don't they try to outguess the pitcher?"

No doubt about it. And now comes the fine discipline of determining a pitcher's "pattern."

Most pitchers, and their catchers who call the game, or the coaches who do the same, are creatures of habit. Observant coaches and players know this and watch the pitcher's warm-ups to see what her favorite pitch is. During the game they will see a pattern develop, and it is this pattern that will eventually destroy even the best pitcher.

Pitchers will invariably work on their favorite pitch more than the others in her arsenal. It doesn't take much of a genius to recognize this. Then, in a moment of crisis in the game, this pitch will be called. After all, it has worked in the past. Why not now? Wham, again!

Game patterns persist. On an 0-2 pitch, many pitchers throw a high and outside waste pitch. They will not do it just once, but every time. Thus, the count automatically goes to 1-2.

On any count where pitchers feel they are in trouble, such as 3-0 or 3-1, they will invariably go to their revered fastball. But as the level of play increases, the skilled batters know this, and they make good use of that knowledge.

The conclusion is conclusive. We all know that variety is the spice of life, but it is also the spice of pitching.

Chapter 17
SO, COACH, YOU KNOW
ALL ABOUT ORTHOPEDICS?

Orthopedic persons, sometimes known as orthopods, deal with human bones. Most of us coaches are not one of these people. We are merely citizens, turned coach, who rely on experience, advice, and a certain amount of witchcraft to ply our trade.

One thing that experience teaches us is that muscles, and bones, particularly mine, need rest. Constant use, without rest, can be detrimental to mind and body. There are probably those who will disagree and feel that hard work, hour after hour, day after day, etc., paves the road to success.

One particular concern relates to softball pitchers. There is a video somewhere that contains language to the effect that to be a good pitcher, one must throw 300 to 500 pitches a day, no matter the age of the child. Not to worry, the film indicates, for windmill pitching is a natural motion and will not harm the arm.

So, believing that practice makes perfect and, for the most part it does, our pitchers begin throwing immediately after the summer season, through the fall, winter, and early spring. The age matters not. It is throw, throw, and throw.

Coaches spur on the pitching hopefuls. Doting parents who have added up college costs and who have been convinced that all

SMITTY SAYS:

After the summer season, have your pitchers take some time off. Let them rest their weary old bones and use their mind for other pursuits. Three or four months off will not hurt performance on the mound. It gets darned boring just practicing, and if this is all that is done for an extended period, a lazy routine develops. Time off will bring enthusiasm back into the hearts and minds of your young players — and just when it is time to get back into the swing of things.

pitchers will obtain automatic, full-ride athletic scholarships to the college of their choice, join them.

The popularity of this notion begat pitching schools, which begat pitching schools, which begat...and these go on all year long.

When the season begins, pitchers throw even more. Not only is there practice between games, but pitchers throw game, after game, after game, particularly on weekends in the summer. Even worse, during the cold spring season, pitchers throw in all manner of conditions, including double headers.

A little math is in order here. Let's see now, take a pitcher who begins throwing 200 pitches, twice a week, beginning in October and ending about March when most high schools begin their practices for the upcoming season. That's five months or about 20 weeks, meaning our pitcher has had 40 workouts of 200 pitches each, totaling 8,000 pitches.

Now, in March the pitcher throws 150 pitches, let's say five times a week for four weeks up to the first of April. That amounts to 3,000 pitches.

So far we have 11,000 pitches, and our pitcher has not played a single game.

Then the high school season begins. In most states it occurs in April, May, and the first week in June. So we have about nine weeks of play.

Let's assume an almost exquisite situation over which most coaches would salivate, namely that there are two good pitchers on the team who divide four games a week. Thus, a pitcher will pitch two games and have, let's say, two practices each week. If she throws only 100 in each game and 100 in each practice, she will throw 3,600 pitches in the season. Her total is now 14,600 pitches.

But, not to worry. Our young pitcher has the summer travel team season left. She might be involved in as many as 80 games in a two-month period.

To be fair, the team our player is on may have two other pitchers. For easy figuring, let's say our pitcher throws in only 20 games. If she throws 100 warm-up pitches and 100 pitches in each game, she will total 4,000 pitches in two months. Include two practices a week for eight weeks throwing 100 pitches each practice and the

summer pitch total rises to 5,600. Added to our preseason practices and high school games, we arrive at a grand total of 19,600
pitches in a 10-month period.

Now let's suppose our pitcher began pitching when she was
eight years old and she is now 18. Then multiply the years times
the number of pitches. You do the math.

How about the really young ones doing this much pitching?
Should we put kids who have not reached puberty through such
strenuous physical activity? Remember, that their muscles and
bones have not as yet developed, and we could be doing more
harm than good to their bodies. Besides, kids need time to be kids.
Are we taking too much time away from this enterprise?

Those who advocate that the windmill motion is "natural" and
that it will not harm a person are living in a dream world. Any
activity that is overdone will have disastrous consequences. Merely
moving one's finger back and forth 200,000 times will more than
likely result in problems with that finger. Joints do wear out, you
know. Ask anyone who has had a knee or hip replaced.

Keep in mind that the above are minimum numbers. Some
pitchers actually throw double this amount, depending upon the
number of pitchers on the team and the amount of required practice. If there is only one pitcher on a team...oh, my.

Certainly, there are those who thrive on this amount of activity. Many a great pitcher has done this and more. Some have even
survived to pitch after reaching 40 or older. But these are exceptions. The vast majority falls by the wayside much sooner.

There is mental fatigue, as well, but we will leave that for the
shrinks. However, the strain and boredom of pitching this much
has to take its toll upon the young psyche.

And the physical effect of all this? Arm and shoulder pain,
aching joints, and back problems are common complaints. General fatigue is routine. And, there is no way to measure the effects
in later life.

We have to hand it to our pitchers, though. If other players
worked half as hard as they do, there would be great improvement on the field of play.

But then, there must be a point of diminishing returns, even
for pitchers. When is enough, enough? Hard to say, but it is clear

that coaches who continue to use one pitcher over and over, day in and day out, with no rest, are asking for trouble. Couple that with an insistence that they pitch for extended periods without physical and mental rest bodes ill for all those involved.

Maybe us coaches should read up on orthopedics. Not a bad idea, eh?

Chapter 18
THE $10,000 QUESTION —
WHY REST?

I love to observe games. Observations can be the greatest of all teachers, if one analyzes the situation being observed, mulls it over, and uses the experiences to become better at one's trade. Few coaches do this and, as a result, our charges — the players — suffer. Games become history when they are over, but the lessons of history are often forgotten. History, itself, is burdened with those who learned nothing from its tutors.

So now I'll tackle blasphemy, that being the criticism of other coaches and their techniques, keeping in mind, of course, that no one, is perfect in any area, much less coaching.

When it comes to pitching, why do coaches constantly overuse their pitchers? "I only have one pitcher" is a lousy excuse. It is your responsibility as a coach to see that your team has other pitchers. Barring injury or sickness that can wipe out a pitching staff in an instant, there is no excuse for pitching one girl, game after game, in doubleheaders, in cold and hot weather, again, and again, and again.

Coach, look at the harm you doing to the pitcher's arm by constantly pitching her without proper rest. Don't, please don't, respond with the idea that the windmill motion is "natural" and won't hurt the arm. Hornswaggle and pitttentoosh! Try bending your index finger back and forth 300 times a day, seven days a week, eight months a year. That's a natural motion too, but you will be seeing your medic before long. You can bet on it.

SMITTY SAYS:

Watch for signs of fatigue, illness, and crotchetiness. These are all red flags warning that your players, perhaps mostly your pitchers, are in need for a little R&R.

Oh, and don't worry about the mental side of using a pitcher constantly. Sure, she likes to be in the limelight and pitch often. Yes, she is looked up to and admired by peers and fans. But, at what cost?

Wouldn't it be nice just to sit out a game or two occasionally, or play another position? Pitchers may not admit it at a tender young age, but as the old body begins to show sign of wear and tear and the pressure of game upon game mounts, they begin to crave a little rest.

The cost of overuse adds up to a bevy of complaints — sore arms, pulled muscles, tendonitis, bursitis, and sundry other ailments that show up periodically when one finally gets to college. It is then that the wear and tear begins to really show up, although there are often manifestations earlier in pitching careers. College coaches want healthy players, especially where scholarships are involved. Overuse of pitchers can take a valuable product and summarily destroy it in furtherance of the urge to win every game.

Positional players are rarely subjected to the same "thinking" as it applies to pitchers. Often, however, there are parents or coaches who believe that rest is a word equal to a losing record. Rest? Heavens to the diamond god, players need play and practice, not rest. Rained out today? Well instead of a day off, let's have a three-hour practice in the gym. That's the sometimes thinking of "there-is-nothing-in-the-world-except-softball" people.

But rain gives our bodies a day to heal from the injuries, great and small, and to perhaps use the time for educational purposes. Education? Yes, that little item that will do more good for our players in the future than all the softball games in the world.

Rain also gives players time for just plain mental relaxation. Rest might even help coaching dispositions, that often take various forms of frightful manifestations.

How come you roster 18 kids, but play only a few, like the best nine or 10? Is winning that important, or don't you like the rest of the team? It is Smitty's law that if you roster a kid, you should play her. Period! Bench sitting for a season is hard on the backside, not to mention the substitutes' mettle and the internal strife that invariably results. Parent problems? You ain't seen nothin' until you sit a kid for most of the season.

Part Five:
BATTER UP!

Chapter 19
KEYS TO THE HITTING UNIVERSE

Hitting is a process that is forever a matter of discussion. Scarce is the coach who knows nothing of the art. It is a matter of universal "knowledge," and any coach who has been in the game a bit will have opinions as to how to master the craft. This is not true with other aspects of the game, such as the mysterious windmill pitching techniques that defy all logic and reason.

Not that all this is bad, mind you. There are many concepts that are universal, basic, and must be implemented if players are to become good hitters. These are found in all good dissertations on hitting, and most coaches are aware of them in varying degrees. On the other hand, there are items that are not discussed. They need to be if we are to have success in getting our batters to hit the ball down and hard.

The direction and velocity of a hit ball are important considerations. They are paired with consternation, often resulting in swinging strikes and fly balls. For example, many batted balls find their way meekly into the appreciative hands of infielders, or they sail harmlessly up into the air and down into outfielders' gloves. Thus, batting averages often witness the debit side of the ledger.

How can these frustrating consequences be overcome, assuming that all the book learnin', talkin', and conceptin' have been digested and put forth to players? Well, there are ways.

The first thing every person who expects to be coaching for any length of time should do is get access to a video camera and a VCR with slow motion. A shuttle for the VCR is a good item, because it allows one to slow down the action frame by frame. Now, what to look for.

The Eyes

Watch a player's eyes. Do they follow the ball to the bat? They should. Have them follow the ball with their nose. Generally, the eyes will follow the nose and prevent batters from losing the ball 20 feet from the plate. Kids understand this concept.

Note whether batters stand at the plate with their heads curiously tilted. If they do, they are getting a distorted picture of an approaching pitch. Have them look at the ball with level eyes.

When waiting for a pitch, do your players turn their heads so that their noses actually block the rear eye? Best that they should see the ball with both eyes. This is especially critical since the back eye can be the dominant optic receiver.

Are your players watching the motion of the pitchers rather than the ball? Many pitchers go through a flock of gyrations as they prepare to deliver the ball. Batters often get hypnotized by these actions and forget their office duties until it is too late.

The Stride

A long stride is a pitcher's friend. To stop this relationship, cut your batters' strides to no more than a couple of inches. It is a fact that one cannot hit a ball well unless the front foot is planted, except in the case a slapper or drag bunter. The longer it takes to stride and plant the front foot, the longer it takes to hit the ball. Some batters eliminate the stride altogether. This is not a bad idea, for it adds to quickness — a necessary batting quality.

Note that if your batters do stride, the hands will come forward with the step, thus eliminating much of their power. If a stride is taken, then ensure that your batters take their hands back as they stride forward. Not easy, but necessary.

Rather than stride, some batters pick up their front foot and set it down as they begin their swing. This is a timing thing, and I would not recommend it. With faster pitchers on the mound, batters simply don't have the time to do ballet maneuvers.

If your batters use a stride, make certain that they stride to the ball and not pull off pitches. This is a common mistake.

SMITTY SAYS:

One key fits best of all to the Hitting Universe — the game of pepper, otherwise known as live batting practice.

The Hands

Take a look at whether your batter's hands get to the top of the ball. They should. Make certain the hands are not dropping just as the swing begins.

The hands sometimes have a triggering action. That is, they move back and up. This is fine, and it is a method used by batters to get ready to launch the bat. Care must be taken not to wrap the bat behind the head.

The first move to the ball must be in a "wood chopping" motion, rather than a wrist roll. The hands are like those of a martial artist attacking an opponent with a karate-like stroke. This is the proper wrist action necessary to hit a ball properly.

Bat extension is a difficult concept to understand, and when batters are told to extend their bats as they swing, they often cast the bat with their hands and become what is known as "arm swingers." Proper extension begins as the batter is making contact with the ball, and then she extends the arms outward in the direction of the hit. It is what is known as hitting "through" the ball.

It is crucial that the hands remain back in the launch position until the very last split second. Batters do not realize how fast their hands are and often get out in front of a pitch by swinging early. They must be taught to wait as long as possible, and then launch their hands with as much force as possible.

The Legs and Hips

Keep the weight back and drive those legs and hips in a violent turning motion as the hands are launched. That is the way to do it, period. Use your VCR to determine if your kids are using their body parts properly.

The Bat Barrel

Use the VCR to see if your players cause the barrel of the bat to dip just before they launch their hands. This is a great cause of fly balls and strikeouts, as the batters tend to swing under the ball. Here, the lower wrist moves out and up and/or the top wrist moves down and in.

Tools

The batting "T" is an excellent device to correct hitting faults. The pitching machine is another. Flip drills are also used. There are fancy devices all over the place to eliminate the stride, promote balance, and prevent other swing faults. They are all useful, albeit costly, but the big problem with them is that you cannot take them into the batter's box with you. Another factor is that even the very worst hitter can adapt to a "T," a machine and flip drills, but they will never hit in a game.

Chapter 20
DOWN AND HARD

There are lots of ways to get on base in softball. Rather than discuss the sundry means, let's talk about the fine art of hitting and some of the things we coaches need to check out.

Let's decide on what we want first. Do we want power hitters who always pull the ball, spray hitters who hit to all fields, or a combination of both, or neither? Neither? Yes, we could employ a short game using slaps, drag bunts, and the like.

Now, our rosters might decide the obvious. For example, little Vivacious Veryweak, who stands five feet two and weighs 90 pounds, will probably not be well-suited to hitting balls off of, or over, outfield fences. On the other hand, Morticia Muscles might be a banner dinger hitter.

To add to our occasional dilemma is the foot speed of our team. It is Smitty's Law that faster players reach base safely more often than slower players. Astute coaches taking note of this law should probably make adjustments in their approach to hitting. For example, a fleet-footed lefty who can drag bunt is a treasure. The same person who can drag and slap adds to the wealth. But a lefty who can drag, slap, and hit with power is a coach's dream.

On the other hand there are kids who are slow because of weight, or they are just simply slow movers. Sometimes we can change the former with some encouragement, although we need to be careful here so as not to encourage the development of more problems with eating disorders. Slow movers can be made a bit faster by better running techniques, but generally they remain slow despite our best efforts.

Whatever, the unmistakable function of a bat on the softball field is quite simple. Other than pounding in base stakes and pitching rubbers, its office is to hit a softball hard, somewhere between the white foul lines. How this is accomplished

SMITTY SAYS:

So, coaches, get used to those time-worn expressions if you want good offensive results, and those are: "Get on top! Down and hard!"

depends entirely upon the person using it and the manner in which it is used. Keep in mind, there will be pitchers and fielders attempting to confound the appointed specialty of the bat.

Every coach in the world believes he/she is a hitting expert. Over and over I have been asked about the various theories of hitting. Every time, without exception, the questioner interrupts and sets forth various personal observations on the subject.

Many times these invectives occur during lectures at clinics. I will be interrupted with a question, such as, "But coach, don't you think a hitter should do this or that?" This is never really a question, but is, by tone of voice, more of a proclamation. If the statement is not immediately acknowledged as a profound truth, rumblings and whispers emanate from nearby compatriots of the questioner. They nod in agreement with the question-statement, and then, in unison, cast disparaging glances in my direction.

This always causes a bit of anguish, because a challenge has been made and must be met. One could argue with the questioner, but that only causes more wretchedness. Reasoning sometimes works, because usually the problem involves miscommunication rather than anything else.

Or could it be that all my years of experience have misled me? Were the greatest of all male and female hitters doing it improperly all these years? But then, I always remember that lo these many years I have paid attention to some of the game's greatest stars, their theories, practices, and writings. By employing these proven techniques, together with a smattering of my own idiosyncrasies and abnormalities, I have been rather contented with the results.

It is Smitty's law that good hitters hit the ball down and hard and that poor hitters hit routine fly balls and weak grounders. If the law is conjured, then good hitters will benefit their teams, while poor ones will hold their heads in shame.

"Down and Hard!" That's the key phrase. We must first agree that it's a necessity for our team. After that, implementation comes into play. So, how do we do this thing, coach?

If the barrel of the bat meets the ball squarely in the middle, generally a line drive will result. This is the best of all possible worlds. Next best is that the barrel hits the top part of the ball, generally resulting in a ground ball.

Now a batted ground ball is nice because even if it happens to come within range of a player it must be fielded, then thrown to another fielder who, in turn, must catch it. Thus, three things must occur, and if one of the elements is missing, the batter will become a runner.

A fly ball, on the other hand, is what I call a "thank-you-ball." Only one thing has to happen and we all know what that is.

A home run over the fence, by the way, is merely a miss-hit single. A line-drive gapper that goes for a home run is a well hit ball. These are two conclusions that must be made if the "down and hard" theory of hitting is used.

So, to accomplish this desired result, a batter must swing the bat down on top of the ball. The barrel must come from the top of the swing and not drop under the ball. Getting players to do this will be difficult, for many things get in the way such as:

- a long stride;
- a drop of the back shoulder;
- a collapse of the knee or hip; or,
- poor hand action.

All will cause the barrel of the bat to drop and generally a disappointing result follows. When there is success, it is probably an accident.

Chapter 21
DOWN FOR THE COUNT

We know there is a strike zone, somewhere between the arm pits and the top of the knees. Coaches work hard to teach their charges exactly where this is located. But it is a drifting concept and depends entirely upon the disposition of the plate umpire, even though the definition in the rule book is quite clear.

Sometimes the strike zone is consistently inconsistent. Coaches would allow that it is not a sometimes thing, but a normal condition. Umpires would disagree. But then, we all have our personal agendas.

Unfortunately, there is no such thing as a DU, or designated umpire, who can be substituted at will by the teams. Nor is there a pinch-umpire, so we must deal with the person who shows up and works behind the catcher, at least for the game at hand.

There aren't enough complications hitting a round object with another round object so that the first round object reaches its objective. Now, we add this zone thing and something called "hitting for count." Will the problems never end?

We want aggressive hitters. No doubt about that. We don't like timid souls at bat. But overly aggressive players sometimes are overly aggressive. Clear? Yes, they tend to overly aggress every pitch. This leads to swinging at bad pitches, getting out on the front foot on change-ups, and generally lousy batting averages.

There is no Smitty's Law on how to take an aggressive hitter who swings at everything and train her to hit "her pitch" or "for count." Although we talk about discipline at the plate and pitch recognition, it is difficult to teach. There are some training aids, such as colored balls, and the like, but there is no magic wand that can be waved to make a batter swing at good pitches. Experience may be the best, and only, teacher.

Once, two clinicians were speaking at a gathering of coaches. The first said that her pitchers seldom throw a ball in the strike zone. The second speaker had just won a national championship and said there were not more than two pitches in the strike zone during the entire last game.

Now, this says something, although it is not clear exactly what. If the clinicians were correct then there should have been lots of walks, but that didn't happen. It would appear, then, that aggressive batters were swinging at bad pitches. Funny, the rule book still states that if a batter gets four balls called, she gets to go to first base.

In fairness to the great pitchers operating on the diamonds these days, it must be said that they have great movement on their pitches, and they are thrown at varying speeds. This, coupled with the outstanding athletes milling about defensively, threatens the .400 batting averages of wannabe Olympians.

But not to worry. There may be a solution. It is called "hitting for count" — a beast that can, indeed, be taught.

Pitchers, who are creatures routinely loathed by batters, tend to want to "get ahead in count." They will invariably try for a strike on their first pitch, national champions to the contrary, notwithstanding. The pitch used will generally be a "fastball." Aggressive hitters, knowing this, normally take a good cut at these pitches.

The intelligent pitcher, coach, or catcher who sees this propensity in hitters will alter the pattern and either throw a ball out of the zone, a breaking ball of some sort, or something else on the first pitch. Batters who want success will recognize the change in the pitcher's pattern and will then begin to hit for count.

A good hitter wants a 1-0, 2-0, or 3-1 count, maybe even a 2-1 count. It is then that a pitcher will try to throw a strike. Really good pitchers may use "stuff" here if they have confidence in their

---

SMITTY SAYS:

It is an absolute that batting averages will be enhanced if batters will try to get ahead in count. It is also a certainty that if they do not, on average, they will go down for the count.

pitches, but these are rare birds. Usually, the pitch used is the so-called "fastball." It is a nice present for the disciplined hitter. It is the "wounded duck" of hitting.

On the other hand, the pitcher may be challenging the hitter by throwing a fat pitch, saying, "Okay, kid, here it is. See if you can hit it and if so, see if you can get it by my defense." This pitch will come more often when a pitcher has a nice lead, since they would rather challenge hitters than to walk them. Walks tend to be rally starters.

The 3-0 count presents a different problem for the coach on offense. Do we take the next pitch or not? This is a coaching decision that must be made. Most coaches will take the pitch. Some will have batters swing if the pitch is fat. The game situation may prevail, but it must be kept in mind that the batter has the advantage here. Further, defenses tend to relax on 3-0 counts, which is not exactly a bright thing to do.

Pitchers love to put batters "in the hole." That is, they favor the counts of 0-1, 0-2, and 1-2. They don't particularly like a 2-2 count, but feel they still have the advantage. It is at these times that hitters are vulnerable to "stuff" — pitches barely catching the strike zone or just missing it.

There is a rule that umpires follow. This rule states that if a batter has two strikes and a pitch is near the strike zone, the umpire must "ring her up." Yes, our umps get a Herculean thrill as they jump in the air, turn around three times, and bellow, "Haaaaaaaa!" Their right arms are thrown upward and outward with such force that one fears dislocation will result. So it would behoove batters to be a bit more aggressive on pitches near the strike zone if burdened with two strikes.

When "in the hole" on counts, batters should move closer to the plate, choke up on the bat, and try to make contact with anything near the strike zone. The zone should be expanded in the batter's mind by at least two inches in all directions; in, out, up, and down.

Chapter 22
WHY AIN'T I HITTIN', COACH?

"Atom" ball, or "at 'em" ball. It's all the same. The batter hits a screamer, a blue darter, a frozen rope, or just a plain old hard-hit line drive. Sorcerers from the enemy conspire every fielding practice to have well-schooled athletes snatch these rockets from the air and turn them into...ugh! Outs!

The player says, "I'm in a slump! I can't hit. Merciful heavens, I'm a failure."

Well, it's fact that seven times out of every 10 a good hitter fails. Six and two-thirds times out of 10 a very good hitter fails, and six times, or less, out of 10 an excellent (nay, even great) hitter fails. Airline pilots during landings, takeoffs, and flights in general cannot afford this failure rate. Nor can brain surgeons. Horrors! But we softball players can succeed only three out of 10 times and be considered good at our trade.

Before we proceed further, let's examine 100 times at bat in 25 games. If we get 32 hits we hit .320. Pretty good. If we get 22 hits, we hit .220. Pretty sad.

Let's see now. The .220 hitter has 10 less hits in 100 times at bat in 25 games, or one less hit every 2.5 games. So, if a player gets one more hit every 2.5 games, she will become a great hitter and a team hero, rather than a "so-so, sort of nothing, and we wish she played on another team" kind of hitter.

It is Smitty's Law that the usual function of a batter, when there is no particular strategic sign given by the coach, is to hit the ball down and hard. Should the batter hit a line drive, so much the better. By doing this, a batter has the best chance of getting on base, percentage wise.

Batters somehow fight this concept. It's not clear why or what the reasoning is. Perhaps it is their inflated batting averages in a weak travel league, where they faced inferior pitching and fielding. This thinking tends to make players believe that they can continue to swing at the ball in the same poor fashion on an upper

---

SMITTY SAYS:

The closer the batter is to the front of the box, the closer she will be to first base. If she stands in the back of the box, you have a teeny tiny fraction of a second more time to see and hit a pitch, but that small amount of time will not make up for the distance you lose to first base.

---

level team and be just as successful. Now, we all know that's not true, don't we?

One day while watching a team taking batting practice, a player hit almost every ball into the air. Some were quite long hits, but none left the park and most would have been routine outs. The hitting coach suggested that the player take 20 swings and try to do nothing but hit ground balls. This was done. Of the 20 hit balls, 14 were screaming line drives, four were hard hit ground balls, one was a routine fly ball, and one was a weak pop-up. The coach opined that based upon the force of the balls that were hit, and allowing for a couple of voodoo-like defensive plays, the player would have had at least 14 base hits for a .700 average.

The coach pointed out that on the previously batted balls, most were routine fly outs, and two were line drives, resulting in a probable .100 batting average, at best. The player was not impressed and asked, "Coach, can I go back to hitting now?" Yes, the player wanted to return to her fly ball hitting practice. Amazing! How do you argue with this mentality?

So we are back to the mental side of hitting. It is the starting place for all good hitters and must be examined over and over during the playing season. Some notions that we, in our roles as coaches, must drive into the minds of our young players are following:

1. Believe in yourself and that you will hit the ball down and hard.
2. Look at the fielders and see "holes," not people, and then visualize a hit going into one of the holes.

3. Be an aggressive hitter who forces the defense to react.

4. Forget the game situation and pay attention to your job.

5. Know that you are working to get on base, with the realization that you can't score from the bench.

6. Know that a hit to the opposite field is just as meaningful as a ball that is pulled and, in fact, if hit to the right side will almost always advance any runners on base.

7. Use the switch in your head to turn off hitting advice while you are at bat, keeping in mind that such is for practice and not game situations.

8. Keep yourself relaxed, like all good hitters do.

9. Watch other hitters, studying their strengths and weaknesses.

10. Keep working hard on your fundamentals.

These are but a few points, which should help your batters. It is axiomatic that you must score to win, but it is equally true that to score you must first get on base, a small detail that is sometimes overlooked.

So, when those hard hits aren't getting through, your player's might ask, "Why ain't I hittin?"

I would say, "You are hittin', kid. You just ain't hittin' for average."

Chapter 23
YIPPITY DOODADS... A FASTBALL!

The hitter steps in...the pitcher fretfully gets her sign, fearful of the menacing figure in the batter's box...

"Hey coach! What should I throw this hitter? They have been rocking me all day. This team has already flattened two Smedley SD13s, and the last one they hit landed on the third diamond north, and, frankly, I'm scared out here."

Whoa! What hitter? She hasn't got a hit yet. Until she does, she is just someone standing in the batter's box with a long, albeit sometimes massive, metal stick.

Meanwhile, the hitter...whoops, the batter...confidently steps in, relaxed, eyes fixed menacingly on the pitcher, feeling certain that she will make solid contact with anything thrown into the strike zone.

The scenario is sometimes reversed. Scared batter...people on base...folks in the stands...pitcher standing confidently on the mound, looking very coercive and malevolent, quite certain that this new batter will soon be history. "Zounds," thinks the batter. "What if I should strike out? The world will surely end!"

Sometimes both pitcher and batter are confident and ready to do battle. Other times, both are insecure and tentative. Age and

---

SMITTY SAYS:

Encourage your players to get to know their bats — the balance and sweet spots. They can only learn this by handling it often. Remind them to play with their bats as they sit on the bench and relax as they hold it in various ways. Have them pay particular attention to their grip, making sure that each time they pick it up, their knuckles are aligned. This way the bat becomes an extension of themselves.

experience play a large part in all this, but coaches will also have a tremendous impact. Let's examine some items, which should help develop proper skills in these components of the game.

Pitchers need to be taught that fastballs, while extremely effective during the formative years in softball, can be a bit bothersome as competition becomes tougher in the later years of one's pitching career. Such pitches, when hit, tend to travel at an outgoing velocity, roughly double that of the pitching speed. If one continues to throw nothing but fastballs, it is wise to wear a suit of space-age armor, and to recruit an excellent outfield skilled in relays.

It is the law of experience, that the faster the pitcher, the more effective an off-speed pitch becomes. Sometimes we call this pitch a change-up, but all this means to most pitchers is a slow fastball. Let's call it off-speed instead, so that pitchers will know that they can use drops, rises, knuckle balls, palm balls, and varying speeds of curveballs, all of which work in the manner of what is commonly called a change-up. Not only that, but they also have great movement. All of these pitches are designed to fool batters, and it is Smitty's Law that a batter fooled is a batter sitting on the bench rather than one standing on a base.

Lesson: speed is nice, but not twice, or too often; off-speed is great, if not used too late, or too seldom. Which brings us to pattern pitchers...

Sage advice given over the years is to pitch in the "L". That is, high in, low in, low out, etc. Good advice. But, even though some batters may look stupid, most know what a bat is for. They come back from the first two unsuccessful times at bat and say to themselves, "Let's see now. During my first two at bats she came hard and high out, then low and out, and then hard and low in. Next at bat she did the same. It would not be presumptive of me to conclude that she might do the same on my third at bat."

Good thinking. Next order of business for the defense: "Set it up! Set it up!" The relay, that is.

So, we will just chart the batters. Ha! That should do it. Looks like Batter X can't hit low, inside pitches. Charts show this. But note that Batter X will have charts too, normally kept in her personal computer between her ears. While the pitcher has been practicing throwing historically effective pitches, Batter X has been reading the book too. Yes, she set the pitching machine for just such pitches and has practiced hitting them through the batting cage net. Next game: "Relay, relay." Oh, you get the picture.

Thinking pitchers work with their thinking catchers. They become bonded and tend to think alike. The relative positions of hitters in the box are studied. Both know which pitches have been effective against which batters and use their memory to mix up their opponents. Patterns must be avoided at all costs. Predictability becomes a liability. Sometimes guesswork and instinct are at work, but then we coaches also engage in the arcane at times, do we not?

Hitters, I mean real hitters work with each other. They study pitchers for patterns. Asks one hitter, "Did she pitch you the same as me, and the same as in the previous games?"

The other replies, "No. She varied the pattern. The first time up she went up and down out, slow down and in. The next high and in hard, then slow high and low out. I expect hard low and out, slow in low and high."

"Too much brainwork for kids," you ask?

Perhaps. We might not want our hitters to do that much thinking in the box. They might do better not trying to outguess the pitching. On the other hand, when an aspirin tablet pitcher is on the mound, a batter may have no choice but to look for certain pitches. But if I am getting jammed all the time and making outs, I may want to look for inside pitches and work hard to get my hips through on them. Finally, it may depend on the hitter. One may be a good hitter if she guesses, but another may not, and she may have to rely solely on instinct and ability.

As with all sure things, there is nothing certain. That's what makes our sport so great. If Hortense Slugger keeps hitting the ball out of the park, it is essential we find a way to prevent this, else we might as well not play the game. And if a certain pitcher keeps handcuffing us, we have to try to defeat her abilities, or just quit when she shows up. Great players and coaching minds lock in on these problems and look for solutions. Therein lie the challenges, and the fun.

Remember, the brain was meant to be used in softball as well life in general, and should not become addled by extraneous matters over which we have no control. But if pitchers continue to toss us fastballs, a category over which they do have control, then we can happily swing away as we shout, "Yippity doodads...a fastball!"

Chapter 24
GET ON TOP

When batting averages slip and scoring opportunities are missed, there have been dreadful violations of one of Smitty's Laws; namely, that when batting in a softball game, it is far better to be safe than out. It is during these times that coaches will sometimes call one or more of their players to the side, and curious conversations will take place concerning the real or perceived reasons for the violations. I would advise handling the situation with a lecture or two.

Bessie Notsogood is perplexed "Coach! Why am I striking out and hitting fly balls all the time?"

You are either missing the ball or hitting it below the center.

"Huh?"

Lecture number one: This is a ball. (Coach: pick up a ball and show it to your player.)

You continue with the lecture. The ball has a top and a bottom even though it is round. If your bat comes too far over or under the ball, you will miss it. If you hit the ball on top, it will frequently go down, and on those occasions where it remains in the infield area, it forces the defense to make a fielding play, which most often includes picking up the ball, throwing, and catching it, each act providing a chance for an error.

If you hit the ball in the middle, a line drive should result, which by most accounts is the best thing for a batter to realize even though it can be caught, albeit usually with some difficulty.

If your swing causes you to hit under the middle of the ball, or near the bottom, it will generally go up. This results in what is known as a fly ball, unless, of course, your swing is powerful enough to propel the ball into an orbit known as a home run. Only one thing has to happen on the normal fly ball for you to be out. A fielder must catch it.

"So far I understand. If I have a swing which results in an upward motion, and if I happen to make contact with a pitched ball, I will usually hit under the ball and drive it in an upward trajectory, giving a fielder an easy chance in most cases. Further, if I hit a line drive, that is good because it has the best chance of getting out of the infield and alighting on safe territory. If I hit a grounder, the defense has every opportunity to make an error. And sometimes ground balls go through the infield resulting in a base hit."

That seems to be the gist of it.

"I suppose this discussion will cause my batting average to go up?"

Maybe, but it could also help the team. Unfortunately, the player goes happily into the batting cage and nothing changes. She either misses the ball or it goes up when hit.

Lecture number two begins with a ball in hand, turning it ever so slowly. Coach then explains that after the pitcher throws the ball, it will rotate, providing it isn't a knuckle ball. This rotation will not only cause the ball to move in various directions, but will often prompt the bottom of the ball to become the top and vice versa, over and over again, as it revolves on its journey to the plate.

"I see now what is happening to the ball, but what can I do to make the ball go down."

You must aim for the top of the ball, dear hitter, no matter the rotation, because that gives you the best chance of hitting it down. If you make a mistake, it will usually be toward the center of the ball, and that is good because you could hit a line drive. The watchwords become: "get on top."

"That's good, coach, but how do I do this 'get on top' thing?

The hands, dear player, the hands. We get on top by throwing the bat head with our hands to the top of the ball. Certain things we do during a swing sometimes keep our hands from getting on top. For example, batters commonly overstride, collapse the backside at the knee or hip, lift the front shoulder, or engage in a variety of physical contortions. Any of these faults cause the bat head, or barrel of the bat, to drop during a swing.

SMITTY SAYS:

Use the pepper game to sharpen your fielding skills, too. When there's nothing going on in practice or a game, grab a bat, a ball, and a couple of players and go to work.

Often, one fault causes another.

"Explain, please!"

Well, if the back knee collapses, the front shoulder will come up. If the back hip collapses, the rear shoulder will drop with it. If the batter lifts the front shoulder, or chicken wings it, the back shoulder will drop. All of these movements cause fly balls or swinging strikes. You've heard the old song about the foot bone connected to the ankle bone, the ankle bone connected to the leg bone, etc? Well, hitting faults can be connected on just a lonely little flaw, like taking your top hand off the bat during a swing, allowing the bat head to drop.

"This is becoming increasingly less clear...all this theory...very confusing. I just want to know how to get this bat head thing to work in my favor."

Cut the stride down. Keep the knees, hips, and shoulders level, and throw the bat head to the top of the ball. Keep your weight back and initiate your swing with your hands while you simultaneously drive your back hip with your back leg.

"So, if I do all this I should get a level swing, which is good, no?"

Not exactly. We often hear of a level swing, but in any series of swings, few are actually level. I've asked advocates of the "level swing" theory how one would swing level at an inside, knee-high pitch. I've never received a defensible answer. What must happen on such a pitch is what should happen on all pitches. Throw the bat head to the top of the ball.

"Coach, I assume you don't actually throw the bat, so how do you achieve this?"

Learn it in the greatest hitting drill of all, namely the game of pepper. Two to five or so players get about 15 feet from the batter, and one pitches a ball underhanded. Using no body movement, except the hands, the batter chops down on the ball in a shortened stroke trying to hit the ball on the ground to each of the fielders in turn. If the batter uses good eye contact along with this drill, she will become a great hitter. Guaranteed!

Pepper is the great, lost tutor for the art of hitting. Take away all your gimmicks, including the stride box, the balance beam, and all those arm and wrist creations that look like medieval torture devices. Play pepper correctly, and it will teach the proper fundamentals of hitting.

So, when the ball keeps going up and the batting averages down, just call the team together and say, "Lecture one." If the problems continue, say "Lecture two." The kids will get a little chuckle, but will understand what to do. The phrase, "get on top," is used in the third base coach's box and is the only hitting instruction that needs to be given during a game. Keeps things simple.

Chapter 25
THE DINGER

Baseball! Ugh! The game's too slow, the players are overpaid whiners, and it's just too slow. Slow! SLOW! Baseball hitters all think they are King Kong and can hit a homer anytime they want. They are always swinging for the fences. It matters not their stature, athletic ability, or percentage of past success. It is a condition insidiously creeping into softball.

One day a baseball coach was working with a batter who continually hit nice fly ball outs to deep center field. The batter was working on lowering his batting average in this manner when the coach said, "Player, for the next ten swings, I want you to hit nothing but ground balls."

The player took 10 cuts and hit seven hard grounders and two line drives, six of which would have undoubtedly gone for base hits. Only one was a fly ball, resulting in what could be a .600 batting average. Not bad.

Guess what the batter asked? He asked, "Coach, can I go back to hitting now?"

This story is not unlike another that took place in front of me at a softball practice. A coach was working with a young hitter, attempting to get her to hit hard grounders. She was doing a fine job of it when her father sloped up and said, "Hey, Samantha, show the coach your home-run swing."

The coach was a firm believer in the "get on top" theory of hitting. That is, the batter should try to hit the top half of a pitched ball. This thought has been around for more than 150 years, give or take, so the coach said, "We want our players to hit singles and doubles, and if not those, then hard ground balls or line drives. Home runs are not really one of our objectives."

The parent was amazed, astounded, and at a loss for words. Not want a home run? What manner of coaching is this?

The coach, seeing the skepticism and disbelief in the parent's face, tried to explain, but to no avail. The home-run disposition reigned.

This attitude develops because of circumstances during the softball player's formative years. A young player, who has some athletic ability, arm-swings a so-called "fastball" in between some poorly coached kids who have been hidden in the outfield because they "can't" play anywhere else. She circles the bases and is greeted by admiring teammates and proud parents. Perhaps she will even get her name in the local paper. The virus festers.

The next time up our player lifts a high fly that is misplayed and "errored" into what a liberal scorer labels a homer. More kudos are heaped upon this newly discovered "power hitter."

"Power hitter," indeed! These types of batters, if allowed to continue in their ill-advised ways of hitting, will eventually allow every known batting fault to occur singularly or in unison as their careers voyage through an ocean of outs and frustration. Coaches will note: head comes off ball; over-strides, arm-swings; steps in bucket; hitches; casts; falls away; falls forward; lunges; and, well, you name it.

Let's set the record straight for your young players once and for all. Smitty's Law avers that any ball that is hit in the air, and, while fair, soars over a fence of some sort, and thus is labeled a home run, is really a poorly hit single. Doubles, triples, and inside-the-park home runs are those singles that go between or past outfielders.

Translation: in general, a home run over the fence (excluding a line drive), or a long fly ball, is a ball that has been hit when the bat has made contact below the center of the ball. And we know, don't we, that we want to hit either the middle of the ball or more toward the top, right? This will give us either a line drive or a ground

---

SMITTY SAYS:

There are undoubtedly more games won with base hits than with homers. So if we work hard getting on top of the ball and forget the fences, everything else being equal (which it never is), results should be smashing (pun intended).

ball, two results which, on average, will give us a base hit and/or move runners.

Let's take a typical situation. Emily Hitter is a good player and she can hit. She has some power and over the season has connected for a couple of home runs, both of which were hits between the outfielders. She has an on-base average of over 50 percent. Most teams have players like Emily.

Now Emily comes to bat with the bases loaded and her team losing 5-0. If she whacks one out of the park, her team would trail by only one run. She has been at bat 100 times and hit two homers. What chance would you give her for hitting her third, even though the pitcher and the fielders are weak? Percentages say she will not hit a dinger.

On the other hand, given these circumstances, what would Emily's chances be of getting a hit, a walk, or getting on base on an error? Much better, no doubt. And if she does come through, as the percentages say she will, at least one run will score and at a minimum, the bases will remain loaded. She also has a good chance to get a ball between the outfielders, and then what? Only good things, on average.

Besides, a home run is a rally killer. If Emily does hit a homer, her team will still need one run, but there will be no one on base. The home run has gotten the pitcher out of trouble, and if her thinking is clear and not muddled by reason of the hit, she will merrily continue to pitch.

On the other hand, if Emily gets a single, driving in a couple of runs, the rally stays alive, and Miss Pitcher will begin nervously glancing in the direction of the bullpen to see who is warming up. The pitching "yips" will gather strength, and Emily's team will use that energy to fuel Mr. Momentum.

But all laws, including Smitty's, have exceptions. There is Miss Crusher who is 5'10" tall, very athletic, and who carries a tree to the plate. If she makes even feeble contact with the ball, she will pulverize it, and it matters not which part of the ball has been hit. These types of players are superb athletes, and they are able to hit dingers because of their ability and training. Their swings are powerful, and they employ all the basic fundamentals good hitters possess. Most of us are not capable of duplicating their feats. That's why they are Olympic athletes and professional players, while the rest can only dream.

There are those that will partially, or even totally, disagree with all this, and that is fine. But I would sure like to schedule some games with you.

Chapter 26
THE EYES HAVE IT

I have pondered the imponderable. Should I get into a battle over the absurd? Should I join a dialogue that concerns whether batters can see a pitched ball hitting the bat when they take a swing? Well, sure. Why not?

Article after article has appeared denouncing the idea that one can see a ball hitting the bat during a swing. It is widely held that the eyes are not focused and cannot follow a pitch that often travels quite rapidly on its journey to the plate. Pictures have been taken to bolster this concept. Further, studies indicate that since batters cannot see the ball meet the bat, they are making an educated guess as to where the ball will be as they swing the bat.

Poppycock, hogwash, and balderdash!

Let's take the case of a skilled third baseman fielding a hard hit, one-hopper about 40 feet from the batter. The ball suddenly, without warning, decides to strike one of the numerous boulders on our playing field and begins to meander over the fielder's left shoulder. Mind you, the ball could be traveling at well over the speed of most pitches, but miraculously, the fielder spears the ball.

Now, this happens quite often with the very fine fielding young ladies currently playing the game. Curiously, whenever such an outstanding play occurs, we all hear the usual comment: "Look what I found." This reflection by the railbirds, opposing coaches, players, and fans sarcastically mocks the great play that just occurred. Interesting that no one sees the eyes of the fielder looking directly at her glove at the moment of the catch.

Must be a miracle. It couldn't be that the fielder actually saw the ball enter her glove. Why, we can use a camera and see that her eyes were not focused. Therefore, the fielder could

SMITTY SAYS:

During batting practice when a batter takes a pitch, a coach or another player should note whether the player watches the ball all the way to the catcher's glove. This is a good way to tell if batters are "keeping their eye on the ball."

not have witnessed the event and her glove must have made an educated guess as to where the ball was going to end up. There certainly are a bevy of smart gloves loitering about the softball diamonds these days.

In any case, I would submit that sharp, errant bounces are much trickier than any of the pitches advancing toward the strike zone. Yet, time after time, fielders seem to nail the little beasties, all the while looking into their gloves.

If we cannot focus our eyes due to the speed of an approaching ball, I wonder at the wisdom of telling our fielders to "look the ball in" as they field it. Seems to be a waste of time if we can't see the ball.

Well, that's not the same as hitting. It's different. Yeah, it's always different, but to be fair, let's talk about hitting.

We examine the photos and talk to the experts who say the evidence proves that batters absolutely cannot see a ball hit a bat during a swing due to the speed of the ball. That is our premise, but it is a false idol...a golden calf...a speculation based upon chicanery. It assumes that unfocused eyes cannot see.

The naysayers have never seen a martial artist take on more than one opponent at a time. While fighting one assailant, these athletes are able to see a blow coming at them from the side and make a counter move to precisely thwart it, even though this blow is advancing toward them at several hundred miles an hour. Yet, their eyes are not focused on the second threat. Someone will have to explain to me how it is that martial artists and softball players can deal with the unseen so adroitly.

All of us can look at one spot and see peripherally to the side. Basketball players do it all the time. Even though they are not focused on a fellow player, they are able to make an exact pass without actually looking at the receiver.

The eyes are the radar of our minds. Our minds control our launching pads, the muscles. Millions of signals per millisecond are constantly sent, received, and acted upon. If the signals are interrupted in any way before an event occurs, the intended results will not occur, as we would like.

The photos of batters hitting a ball do not lie. They prove the eyes are not focused at impact. Yet, our eyes see. We are not focused exactly on a pitch, and we are not conscious of the moment of impact due to the speed involved, but our minds see the ball through the radar of our eyes and our muscles react accordingly. If this were not so, a pitch that suddenly breaks near the plate would never be hit. There is no way we could make contact if we did not in some way witness the movement, and yet contact occurs on a regular basis, now doesn't it?

Brave souls who do not believe that the ball can be "seen" hitting the bat should close their eyes (if they dare) when the ball is a few feet from the plate and see if their "educated" swing enables their bat to make contact with the ball. Good luck!

Actually, the argument is moot and should never take place. We will never prove it one way or the other. What is important is that we tell our batters to attempt to watch the ball all the way to the bat. If they do this, noses will stay down where they belong, and our batters will stand a better chance of making solid contact.

Forget the argument that a batter cannot see the ball hit the bat. Trust that it can be done and forget about further discussion. Such discourse takes up valuable time which we simply cannot afford to waste. Fundamentals await! The eyes do, indeed, have it.

Chapter 27
TO SAC OR GET SACKED?

SAC stands for sacrifice. When we speak of it in the game of softball, we are normally speaking of a bunt that moves our runners along, although for some silly reason, fly balls that advance runners from third base to home are similarly titled. Now the gurus, located somewhere in softball never-never land, have ordained that the lefty who slaps at the ball and advances a runner is also to be credited with a SAC. Carried to the extreme, which ain't far away, why not credit a SAC to anyone who makes an out advancing a runner? Hey, we could all bat .800, no?

It is incumbent upon coaches to explain to their charges exactly what a SAC is supposed to do. Simply put, it is to give up one's turn at bat to advance a runner in the interests of the team. The object is not to get to first base, although that is a plus, but to insure the bunt is down. Now, this still may not go over better than a lead balloon, but it will pave the way to the next project — that being to convince the team that this is very important. Of that, they are not always sure, to be sure.

Once the purpose of the sacrifice bunt is explained, it is time to instruct the player in the how-to-do-it format. The grip is important, of course, but it is a matter of some controversy due to the fact that we are all human. Whatever grip is used, it must be firm and not in the fingers of the top hand like a baseball player. Remember, a softball bat is lighter and smaller than the one used in baseball, and a baseball is much smaller than a softball. The result is that the mass of the softball hitting the bat will literally take the bat out of the hands of hitters unless their grip is firm. Foul balls and little pop flies result with a loose grip.

So, we choke up a few inches, and place the top hand about midway on the bat, using a very firm grip. Now we are ready for the stance, another point of contention.

Batters usually use one of three stances. They square up to the pitcher with the right foot a tad forward; they pivot at the waist; or, they bunt from a 45-degree angle to the pitcher.

The square stance gives the batter a good sight picture of the ball, but care must be taken as the movement is made to bunt so as not to step out of the box or on the plate with the back foot. This stance gives the batter good balance, but does not allow for a quick start.

The pivot is easiest of all to learn and eliminates stepping out of the box. Its disadvantage is that the batter does not have good balance, has a poor view of the ball, and is inhibited in getting a good start toward first base.

I prefer the 45-degree angle stance when sacrificing. This involves the batter moving merely the front foot a few inches away from the plate while keeping the back foot planted. There is no danger of stepping on the plate, and the stance puts the batter in an excellent starting position. The bunter gets a great view of the pitch.

The angle stance allows the batter to easily prepare for different types of attacks, namely: to sacrifice; to slap; to take a full swing merely by moving the front foot to a normal hitting position; to drag bunt; to fake a drag bunt; fake a swing; and, then to actually bunt; to slug bunt; and to push bunt. The other stances make it more difficult to do these things.

Whatever stance and grip are used, the bat should be held at the top of the strike zone. It is absolutely a no-no to go up for a pitch. This normally results in a miss or an easy pop fly. To go down, the bunter should use the knees, not the bat. Too many kids take only the bat down, and this helps defeat their intended mission. Worse yet, a bat in this position exposes a bunter to a foul ball in the face, something which is not pleasant.

Let's avoid this foul ball thing and up our chances of a good bunt. How? Well, we must first get our sight picture of the ball over the top of the bat by looking directly over the barrel as we assume the bunting position. This relationship between barrel and our head never changes, no matter where the pitch goes. Remember, we never go up for a ball. If we go down, we do it with the knees, not the bat. This is a time-honored technique used for well over a century by good bunters.

SMITTY SAYS:

Keep in mind that the opposition will SACK those who fail to SAC. So get with it, coach. Move those runners!

While bunting, many batters tend to move their bodies toward the ball as it approaches the plate. This is not good. One must allow the ball to come to the plate and sort of "catch" it with the bat, cushioning the blow by giving with the arms. This allows for a soft bunt, which, when done correctly will end its journey about 10 or 15 feet from home plate.

We often speak of "getting on top" when referring to hitting. The same is true in the short game. We must get the ball down and the only way this can be done is to bunt the top of the ball.

The direction of the bunt can be controlled simply by slightly moving the bottom hand. Righties pull it in a bit for a bunt to third and push it out a tad for one toward first base. Lefties do the reverse. But how do we decide which?

The toughest bunt to field and play is one near the third base chalk line. It makes for the longest throw, but often the ball will go foul. This is okay if we want to drag bunt, but if we are sacrificing, we want the ball to be fair. If the pitcher is a lousy fielder, and there are many of these, bunt it directly to her. If not, try to put it toward the shortstop or second baseman. Oh, well, just get it down in fair territory! That's the real challenge, especially if the pitcher throws moving aspirin tablets.

Chapter 28
THE WAY TO THE TROPHY TABLE

Game watching, particularly involving amateur softball, is a splendid endeavor, usually free or at a nominal cost. It is often dramatically exciting. Watching different coaches run their strategies is one of my favorite pastimes, particularly since I believe strongly in a robust offense.

To succeed, a tenacious offense requires that pitches be hit. No colossal revelation, I'd wager. Moreover, batted balls must be line drives or hit hard on the ground. Pop-ups and fly balls do little offensively and are but gifts to the defense.

At times, we must give a great pitcher her due. It is a given that when a pitcher is "on," batters will have difficulty. It is one thing to say that our team was not hitting during a particular contest. It is quite another to say that we weren't hitting because there was a girl on the mound throwing aspirin tablets, and we were unable to solve her mastery. We must occasionally admit that someone actually beat us.

That does not mean we should give up when a fireballer or junker shows up and starts "voodooing" us. That's merely one obstacle facing batters. Another includes fielders who have a habit of appearing from nowhere to magically snatch well-hit balls out of the sky.

A further stumbling block comes from the very slow pitcher and the resulting mentality of: "We can hit fast pitching, but we can't hit the slow stuff." This is a real cop-out, if there ever was one, and it is a tiresome invective. The other inane excuse for losing is that "We gave the game away." Doesn't anyone ever simply lose a game?

We, as coaches, must prepare our teams for all kinds of pitchers and defenses. This is essential if we are to succeed offensively. One of Smitty's laws holds that any team that scores infrequently will generally not have a noteworthy winning percentage.

Although there are "duck-snorts," "Chinese liners," dribblers and other flukes, usually a hard-hit ball is what gets us on base. If coaches want textbook stuff on how to do it, they can go to the library and check out sundry books. There they will find standard advice on grips, stances, strides, etc., which have been around for eons. All are generally good techniques and normally must be employed if one is to hit the ball at all. There are some subtle nuances, however, which deserve attention in detail.

We must make sure our hitters (pitchers and fielders, too) know what we are talking about when we are engaged in the fine art of instructing those who will be handling the bats. Young or inexperienced players do not always know what we are talking about. This often leads to frustration and poor performance. Make yourself understood, coach!

Now, communication involves other things, too. It is one thing to tell a player something and quite another to have that player execute what was explained. We coaches sometimes think a player is inattentive or unwilling to learn, but we should realize that sometimes a player's mind and body might not be in sync.

We can show a player what we mean by demonstration, or, if too ancient or feeble to perform it ourselves, we can have a player take on the task. Sometimes even this will not work, so we must then physically manipulate the player's arms, feet, or body through the motions. The player will then actually have a feel for it. Be careful though. Touching can be misinterpreted, so it is best to explain exactly what you are doing and what you will be touching prior to the demonstration. It would be prudent to have another coach around, too.

For example, when working on holding the bat prior to a swing, physically locate the bat where you want it. Then have the player drop the bat, pick it up, and assume the batting positions several times.

If you want to demonstrate how to move a bat through the strike zone, take a player's hands and move them slowly through the hitting area. Do this several times, then add the bat. Have the player execute this several times on her own and have her do it each time you practice for a couple of weeks.

SMITTY SAYS:

Diligence and attention to the little things will pave the way to the trophy table. Do not count on anything else, for to do so will send you packing before the championship game.

If a player is not hitting well, look at her eyes. Stand at the side and notice how poor hitters tend to stare through the ball, beginning about 10 or 20 feet in front of the plate. Once they have lost eye contact with the ball, contact with the ball becomes sheer guesswork. Not the best of all possible worlds for a batter is it?

To correct this problem, have someone pitch to hitters, reminding the hitter to merely watch the pitch into the catcher's glove. To assist in the process, have the hitter follow the ball with her nose. Generally, the eyes will go along with the nose, and we will obtain our desired result. Training the eyes in this manner will result in a shoulder-to-shoulder head turn, which is precisely what we want.

Most often, we attempt to determine what is wrong with a hitter by examining the swing. Rather, try watching the players when they take pitches. You will see lunging, poor eye contact, forward or upward movement of the front shoulder, hands into the bucket, and of course, tension. These are but a few of the subtle things that should be examined to insure that our batters are making solid contact. Sometimes, correcting one minor flaw in a swing can produce a bevy of hard-hit balls.

Chapter 29
TAKE IT FROM ME

I would like to address a little known and probably misunderstood softball rule. Hitters get only three strikes. Just three! This rule has been around for a long, long time. It is not a new rule invented to drive coaches crazy. It is an old rule, contrived probably in the interest of fairness, since the batter has the advantage of going to first base when the umpire says, "Ball four." But, for some reason, the rule seems to be unimportant, ignored, or just plain forgotten at times.

As an aside, one wonders why, in the interest of fairness, a batter should not get a walk on a ball three count, since that would seem to even things up. Or maybe four strikes should be allowed. But those are matters for another day.

Back to the "strike three" rule. It goes hand in hand with two statements: 1) "A walk is as good as a hit." and 2) "We can't hit." These pontifications are profound and have given rise to the "take" sign, employed by visionary coaches who deem that they are able to foresee the future.

Now the "take" sign was invented to assist what I call nonoffensive-minded teams to get some base runners. The theory is that if the sign is given often enough, the pitcher will eventually walk a batter. Then we can bunt her to second, hope for a wild pitch, and finally, bring her home on a delay during an infield out. Then our "heater," Miss Aspirin Tablet, will take care of the rest.

This theory of offense is used in games even when the opposition's flame thrower is in the seventh inning with a 10-run lead and has displayed excellent control. Apparently, there is the notion that our plan of using multiple "take" signs will tire her out, and she will begin walking batters like crazy, thus allowing us to catch up.

Now comes the "we can't hit" excuses. Well, first off, if a pitcher is "on," you aren't going to get many hits. There are, of course, other reasons for failures at the plate, but one of the big ones has to do with our friend, the "take" sign. In fact, this little gem may be a culprit for the myriad of problems that arise when we do take a swing.

But what if we use the 10-run deficit to enhance our hitting? What a marvelous time to start swinging away! Our hitters have a chance to practice against a good pitcher, to learn the strike zone, and to learn to hit for "count." Our players might even enjoy themselves, albeit they are considerably behind in the fray.

The "take" theory is so prevalent that one would think there is a rule in softball that a batter is not allowed to swing until she has one strike. Some moons ago, I became more educated in the game and learned that this was not a rule, but an offensive strategy, used by many of the great gurus in the third base coaching box.

At some point during my coaching career, I became more curious about this leading theory and decided to reject it. I instructed my pitchers to throw a meatball right down the center of the plate on every first pitch to every batter until they began swinging at it. To the delight of the pitching staff, they found that they now were obtaining an advantage in that the opposition was in an eternal black hole, dug by their coach, that effectively helped take the bat right out of the hands of batters.

Conversely, I taught my batters that they truly were allowed three strikes, and not just the two to which they had become accustomed. They all smiled at this concept and asked, in concert, "Does this mean we can hit any pitch we like, even a 3-0 pitch, coach?"

Yes, you can swing at any pitch you like, when you like, as often as you like, up to the limitations imposed by the rules of softball. You may even swing at a 3-0 pitch, for you will notice that during these moments, the defense tends to relax and Miss Lala will groove a meatball for you. Heck, might even call a "hit and run" on 3-0. That would shake them up, wouldn't it?

Curious expressions of what some might think evilness furrowed the brows of my hitters. They began to salivate at the mere thought of a turn at bat. Thought they, in congruence: Wow! This is what all those other coaches were talking about when they used the phrase "be aggressive." They used the term, but then showed

---

SMITTY SAYS:

As an experiment, try a season limiting use of a "take" sign. See if there isn't an improvement in your batting averages. Bet there will be.

---

us how not to be aggressive by putting on the "take" sign. How quaint.

Yes, by using the "take" sign ad nausium, we do take the bat out of the hands of our hitters. Such coaching sends a message to batters that the coach has no confidence in their hitting ability. Since pitchers these days are getting better and better, and since they are quite capable of throwing a strike whenever they like, taking pitches quite often puts a batter in a one-strike hole, exposing them to the variety of "stuff" that pitchers use nowadays.

If, on the other hand, batters are allowed to look for their pitch, usually one out over the plate about belt high, while using the entire "count," their hitting will improve markedly. Great hitters often take a pitch on purpose, merely to judge a pitcher's ability, speed, etc. Usually, it is the first pitch during the first time at bat. From then on, such batters look for a pitch in their personal "wheelhouse." Beware of such players, for they appear almost indestructible at bat.

Proud of my "new" approach, I engaged a "take-lots-of-pitches" coach in a bit of a chat. He used the "take" sign to teach his batters which pitches to hit.

Astonished, I asked how they were able to learn to hit by taking pitches.

"Well, if they take pitches, they might draw a walk."

I pointed out that the response skirted the question.

"What I mean is that if we need a runner and the pitcher is wild, we will put the 'take' sign on."

So then, the "take" sign is used only in special circumstances?

"Yes."

Well, that conversation certainly limited the use of the rapscallion sign. To be sure, the "take" sign is not totally valueless. Absolutely not. It can be used to get a count for a hit and run, a squeeze, or to check the defense in certain situations. It can be used on a 3-1 count with two out and runners on base, looking for a walk, or a 3-2 count that provides an automatic hit and run situation. There are other uses, as well, but each coach must decide when to use the strategy.

One of Smitty's laws states emphatically: a walk is not as good as a hit. Kids should be at the plate aggressively looking to whack the ball into orbit (actually, hit a line drive or a hard ground ball). Anybody's grandmother can learn to take a walk. That's no trick. Why do we give players a bat? If we are at the plate to walk, then a bat is unnecessary. A fly swatter will do. Take it from me.

Chapter 30
HUSTLE... THE NAME OF THE GAME

When I was playing the game of baseball as a youth, I rode my bike to the ball diamond, arriving about three hours before game time. No one else was there and I wondered why. About 45 minutes before the game, my teammates would arrive, with the opposing team coming 15 minutes later. All strolled to the field, shirts out, stirrups in disarray, and generally in a slovenly manner.

Now, I love the game. I think it's great. I do not respect anyone who plays or coaches the game and who does not cherish it as I do. Unrealistic and unfair? Certainly, to a degree. But then why engage in something if it is an unpleasant experience? Too many players and coaches involve themselves in the game and then go through periods of depression, the doldrums, and self-pity when things don't go as planned. They simply ain't havin' any fun.

During this past season I was at a field and watched a team get off a bus. Slovenly? A compliment. Hustle? Not a hint. They played in the same tacky manner. The team was there for something other than softball. The coaches exhibited a similar attitude.

There are things we cannot control, but hustle is not one of them. As coaches, we must make the demand for hustle, so too must the players demand it of themselves and their teammates. And, of course, all must be aware of the definition of hustle.

What is the definition? Should players merely jog on and off the field, run after errant softballs, and talk it up during play? This is more the common definition of hustle and most players understand it as such.

My definition differs. It includes many things. The first is pride in appearance and conduct. A spirited, hustling team will

SMITTY SAYS:

Great hustle will make your coach sit up and take notice. It is one of the first things college coaches see when scouting teams. You can bank on it.

come to the field dressed sharply, on the run, and will enthusiastically be looking forward to the impending competition. Equipment will be in prime condition and will be handled with care. If not clean, the bench area will be immediately groomed and prepared for equipment and players. After the game, it will be left in the same condition. Personal gear will be dealt with in a like manner by all.

As the well-prepared, hustling team takes to its pre-game activity, it will do so at slow trot, which will gradually increase in pace as muscles begin to warm. Team stretching begins with enthusiasm and gusto, after which there is vigorous sprinting and throwing. Infield practice takes on a similar character.

When the game commences, a hustling team takes to the field at an all-out sprint. This accomplishes several things. It provides base-running practice. It gets players in position to receive more practice fly balls, grounders, and throws. It impresses umpires, spectators, and the opponents.

When coming off the field, hustling teams use the same hard sprint. This gives them more base-running practice, more time to get in and take practice swings, more time to watch the opposing pitcher, and it continues to impress those who are watching.

A spirited hitter will run hard to, and through, first base on all infield grounders and foul balls. After a strikeout, the first move of these hitters is a move to first base, until such time as they become aware that the umpire has ruled them out.

Why do hustling hitters sprint hard to and through first base, even though a ball might be foul? Easy. This is an opportunity to practice running to first under game conditions. Players should always use such opportunities to practice their techniques. If they do not run or pull up short on routine outs or fouls, they have shortchanged their team and themselves. Not only have they lost a practice run, but a "foul" ball may roll fair or a first baseman might drop the ball.

Defensive players who hustle can also use routine situations to sharpen skills during a game. A third baseman, for example, on a ground ball hit foul, can go ahead and make a play, providing an opportunity for a practice throw under game conditions. A pitcher can continue with a pitch even though a batter suddenly steps out of the box. After all, the ump might not have called time, and even so, it is a free practice pitch. An outfielder can practice sacrifice fly techniques on routine fly balls and can fire the ball in to bases each time there is a hit. A foul ball down the left field line gives the fielder a free opportunity to round off a ball, charge it, and come up with a good practice throw.

Games provide excellent opportunities to hone skills, and players should take advantage of such situations, which are free of charge in fee or time. They are available during almost every inning and out.

Maybe hustle is not the term for all this. Maybe it's just enthusiasm for the game, the thrills, the competition, the spectacle of watching great amateur athletes compete. However, I do believe it all begins and ends with hustle. Add the ingredients of enthusiasm and love of the game to that soup pot, and the recipe for success begins to bubble.

Part Six:
THE HEAD GAME

Chapter 31
WHAT'S THE JOB?

Bottom of the seventh. Two out. Bases loaded. Big game. Two runs down. A young batter approaches the plate, more than a bit apprehensive. She thinks: "Big game. What if I make an out? I have to get a hit!"

Mom turns her head, thinking: "I can't bear to watch. What if she would make an out?"

Dad is paranoid. He paces about, thinking: "Gosh, she has struck out three times already today. What if she strikes out now? I would be so embarrassed. How can I ever look the other parents in the eye? Oh well, if she strikes out, it's the coach's fault anyway. He changed her style of hitting, and she hasn't hit a lick since. Bonehead coach!"

The railbirds opine out loud, "Lousy swing. Someone ought to teach her to hit. Coach is a jerk. Can't teach hitting. Should put in a pinch hitter. Parents are jerks. Put too much pressure on the kid."

Chloe Slugger digs in at the plate, preparing to hit. The pitcher gets her sign. The situation is electric.

Railbirds thinking: She can't hit her hat size.

Coach, assuming a Socrates like stance, yells out revelations of logic and counsel, "Come on now. We need a hit. Don't overstride. Keep your eye on the ball. Swing level. Hit it somewhere."

Dad, pontificates aloud, "Don't swing at a bad pitch. Keep your backside arm up. Watch the ball. Watch the pitcher's release. She ain't nothin'. You can hit her."

Mom covers her eyes, but opens a peephole in her hand, and groans, "Aaaaaaaaaaah!"

Strike one!

Comments from all sources persevere.

Strike two!

Ditto.

Strike three!

SMITTY SAYS:

Pragmatically speaking, it comes down to this. What's the job? Well, if we coaches have done our job, our players will more than likely recognize what their job is and will do it quite well. Always? No, but you will often be pleasantly pleased with the results.

Mom thinks: I knew it! She hides her head.

Dad proclaims, "Terrible! Just terrible!" He looks around to see who might be watching.

Railbirds bandy knowing looks about, and shout, "She'll never make it."

Coach, scowling, throws his hat and laments, "Shoulda put in a pinch hitter. She's zero for June."

Suzie wonders: Where can I hide? She throws bat and helmet and then stalks off to the bench.

This scenario is an every day occurrence in athletics. It is repeated for fielders and holds true for pitchers in what are perceived to be important situations where tension is elevated to extremes. Things are bad enough in routine situations, but when the nitty becomes gritty, pressure mounts and situations become tense.

Tense situations? What are these? Well, they are those cases when most of us believe that the situation is critical and that performance must be perfect. But Smitty has another law: Situations in softball should not create tension.

Moreover, there is no such thing as a big game, time at bat, fielding play, or pitching situation. All are important. Worrying about the adversary or the impact of a game causes coaches and players to overlook important matters. Their focus should be on their respective jobs. For the coaches, it is to coach the game, and for the players, it is to execute fundamentals. Another of Smitty's laws says: The opposing team shows up on game day for only one purpose, and that is to beat you.

Therefore, we must teach our players to do the job at hand, which is simply to execute fundamentals. Let the other team worry about mundane matters.

We return to our case of the batter and the bases loaded. Assuming the situation does not call for a specific strategic move, such as a bunt, the job of a batter is to hit the ball hard, preferably down or as a line drive. This role never changes, no matter the inning, number of base runners, score, number of outs, opponent, or the importance of the game. The only important thing is the batters' job, as defined. Everything else is meaningless and should never be allowed to impact the game.

Should the batter hit a line drive directly at a fielder who catches the ball, the batter has done her job. There is no more to say. Many batters feel they have failed in this situation. NOT! They have succeeded! The fact that the hard hit ball did not fall in for a base hit is not in any way, shape, or form material as it pertains to the batter's performance. Does it affect the game? Certainly! We lose, but only because someone on the other team did their job and not because we failed.

This concept is crucial. It applies to all players. The situation does not alter the job of the athlete, which is simply to execute fundamentals. We must do everything possible to get this concept across to our players.

Let's examine the bases loaded situation from a defensive standpoint. Coach yells out, 'Coming home for the force and then first for the double play!"

Now, I would not be totally taken aback if the fielders, unless very young and inexperienced, were not already vaguely aware of what needed to be done. But now the coach has introduced exact instructions into the already 'tense' situation.

Suddenly, a sharp grounder is hit to the shortstop's right. The third base runner goes on contact, and there is no chance to nail her at the plate. But the shortstop has just been instructed to throw home, hasn't she? So she does. Safe! Bases are still loaded and the situation is even more 'tenser.'

If our shortstop knows how to play her position reasonably well, we can probably count on her to make the right play in most cases. In our example, she might choose either to go to third or first base, depending upon her instincts. Unless the run on third were the winning run, the results would no doubt be more favorable than in the example.

Young minds are capable of almost anything given proper guidance. Conversely, if these minds are filled with meaningless or confusing information, they will often fail in critical circumstances causing less than desirable results.

Having coached in state and national championships, it would be idiotic for me to say that I have told my teams that these games are meaningless, and they should be considered 'just another game.' What group of players would, or could, believe this? Obviously none. But every attempt should be made to keep emotion at bay and to focus on the execution of fundamentals.

Chapter 32
PRESSURE IS FOR TIRES

If you were to ask several softball players what is going through their minds in certain situations that, on the surface, are perceived by them to be clearly dissimilar, you would get some interesting responses. The responses would reflect their respective parent and coach training tainted by perceptions from peers. Let's examine three such situations.

Situation 1: A hitter is at bat in the first inning with no one on base and no one out. Situation 2: The same, except a runner is on third base. Situation 3: The same except it is the bottom of the seventh inning and the winning run is on third base. Question: In the mind of the batter, is there a difference between the three regarding her job?

Universally, players will say there is a difference; that Situation 3 is the most important: next is Situation 2; and that Situation 1 is the least important.

Submit the questions to coaches and parents and notice the results. At first you will detect the necks thrusting their heads menacingly toward the questioner, as if they were responding to someone who had attacked their home, family, and flag. They will at first exclaim, "You idiot! Of course there is a differennnnnnnnnnce!" Suspecting a trick question, they will then vainly try to cover up their true beliefs, which are clearly the same as those expressed by the players.

Think about it for a moment and analyze what you have witnessed over the years and what you, yourself, may have done or said as a parent or coach had our imaginary batter lined out, or even struck out, in all three instances.

If the event occurred in the first inning, you would hear, "Nice try. Don't worry about it. Get 'em next time."

In the second situation, coaches and parents, being disappointed with the result, will act a bit sullen, but they get over it in varying degrees depending upon whose kid was at bat, the perceived importance of the game, and the scouting reports about the enemy — its importance and competence.

The third situation elicits the true beliefs of those involved. Whether actually stated in so many words or by reactions such as dirt kicking, helmet throwing, and appropriate brooding and scowling, the universal response is: "That cost us the game! We can't hit! That out beat us!"

Clearly, the third circumstance is held to be the most important of all, and to all. So, we send mixed signals to our kids which go like this: If you make an out in the first inning with no one on, it's okay. If you do it in our second situation, you are sort of okay, but not really. If you do it with the winning run on third in the seventh inning, you are a bum.

Now, look at the situation in reverse. If you get a hit in the first inning, you are just okay; a little better in the second situation; but if the hit occurs in the seventh with the winning run being plated, you are a hero!

Imagine! Our batter sends a scorching line drive into the third baseman's glove, and she is either a hard luck hitter or a bum, depending upon the game situation. So, each of our kids will forever say the third situation is the most important.

Remember that these are routine situations. We have taught our batters to hit the ball down and hard. We know that good pitchers and defenses try to keep our batters from doing their jobs. We have told our kids to do their very best; that they should always give 110 percent (whatever that means); and that as long as they do that, all will be well. But our examples indicate that all is not always well, right? Talk about mixed messages.

Other examples include pitchers who fail in so-called tense situations where the next pitch is "the most important pitch of the game." Then there is the fielder who makes an error "at the worst possible time and it cost the game." Oh, don't mention that prior to their derelictions, the pitcher was brilliant over the course of the game or the fielder made great play after great play. The fact that both failed "when it counted" is the significant fact.

When it counted? Didn't it count during the rest of the game? Were those great pitches and plays in the field not important before? What gives here?

SMITTY SAYS:

Pressure can never be eliminated, but it can be eased a great deal. In summary, save pressure for the tires on your car.

What is critical is that kids understand that all game situations and all games occupy equal status regarding importance. None takes precedence over another. It is nonsense to to say, "This is the most important moment in the game." Equally idiotic is the expression, "This is the most important game of the year." And thus, "The pressure is on."

Nothing could be further from the truth as this is pressure put on kids, inspired by parents, coaches, and fans. It causes our kids to freeze in the so-called "moments of truth."

During televised golf matches, announcers are forever commenting on the importance of a putt on the last hole of a tournament. Had the golfer attended to the other putts during the round, this last would not have been elevated to that high office. The same is true with a pitcher when the count is 3-2 and the bases are loaded. To say that this pitch is more important than say the 2-2 pitch sounds a bit much. Are we to believe that pitches become more important as a batter goes deep into the count? Surely not.

It is interesting to note that people driving by the ballpark really are not too concerned with that which is happening in our games. The news media is not frothing at the mouth competing to report our games. Few in the world are much concerned about what happens on our field of dreams. It is only we, our players, their friends and relatives, who are really concerned. And then, once the game is over, it is soon forgotten, even by the winners, only to be recalled in fleeting moments of reflection.

So pressure is a self-imposed sort of thing, brought about at the direction of others. Kids need to be coached on how to focus their attention on the execution of fundamentals, no matter the game importance, the inning, or the score.

Chapter 33
WHICH TEAM SHOWED UP?

Conversations amongst coaches usually revolve on the success of the season. The one I had with Coach MacNonameski is one I could have had with any number of coaches. I'll share it with you:

Well, how's your team doin' this year?

"Depends on which team shows up," said Coach MacNonameski.

How's that?

"Well, one game we look like the best thing since apple pie and the next we couldn't beat the Diminutive Orphans of the Wretched. I just can't understand it, and also, I just can't stand it!"

But coach, you have all the horses. You recruited the best players in the area and some out of the area. They are studs. They are the very best. How can you possibly lose when you have all that plus fabulous funding? It is a mystery to me.

"When you find out the answer to that one, you and I can write a book and we will make a fortune."

After the coach's departure, I searched the deep recesses of my computer-like memory for answers to his dilemma, but for the longest time kept getting messages like: "No such directory on file," or "Bad command or file."

I thought at first I had formatted my memory bank, but lo, while searching the Arcane Directory I located an innocent looking compendium called "Which Team Showed Up?"

Ah, yes. According to my file, many coaches often sailed in the same boat as our confused mentor. This boat sometimes had no

---

SMITTY SAYS:

Which team showed up? Well, since you are the judge, why don't you be the jury and render the verdict too? Passing sentence is the real trick.

mast, sails, tiller, or bottom, and sank awkwardly in most any sea. Yet, on many occasions, it was a veritable Man O' War!

Translation: Teams often play splendidly one game and lousy the next. Sometimes, it is inning to inning or even out to out, but generally, teams go for several games of greatness, followed by the most ghastly and frightening of circumstances. Why?

I have a few theories. No doubt you expected as much. In any case, if we examine the monster we have assembled in our softball laboratory, we might get a few answers.

Take the situation where there is tremendous intensity during a long, extra inning game. It matters not whether the game is won or lost, it is very difficult to get a team "up" for a game that follows. Often, teams who put up a great fight in the long game, end up getting pulverized in the next one. Or what about the game against the Nuw Yurk Yankers, a great team, that we demolished, followed by a loss to a bunch of nobodies? Explanation?

Emotions! Perhaps that is the secret. Are we too emotional during a game? Do we have those peaks and valleys that get us "up" one minute and "down" the next? Are we enthused when something good happens in the game and then demoralized when things go wrong?

Let's look at a simple situation. A ground ball is hit to an infielder. It is routine. It takes a great big, buddy-buddy hop into the player's glove. But horrors! She bobbles it and the runner is safe.

The infielder is a very capable player and has been drilled extensively. Practice after practice she has routinely fielded all such ground balls in a flawless manner. Why now, all of a sudden, without warning, in a game of either no consequence, or one of great importance, does she suddenly violate all basic fundamentals and boot the ball?

Then the error virus strikes another player, then another, until it becomes an epidemic. These are called innings from hell. We've all been there.

Now, the team is very capable. They have trained well. But there may be problems at home we know nothing about. Maybe there's been some great tragedy. Possibly the team had little sleep the night before or there is infighting over boyfriends. The team may be putting pressure on itself to do well. Coach may have yelled too much or chewed the team out too violently. "Could be" encompasses a wide area of possibilities.

Whatever the reasons, it is Smitty's Law that a bobbled ball is a bobbled ball. Reasons for misplays abound, and practice is the place to instill remedies. But to sit around and ponder the imponderable should not be the bane of the coaching staff. Hand wringing should be left to shrinks and mountain gurus. Coaches have better things to do.

As much as we humans hate to admit it, we are human. As such we are prone to be a bit imperfect at times. Some of these times include routine bouncing balls that we ordinarily handle blindfolded. But horrors, again! We sometimes boot them with eyes wide open.

The same things occur when players are at bat or on the mound pitching in a crucial situation. I recall a pitcher at a national tournament throwing a wild pitch and getting to the plate in a most lazy manner so that the tying run scored. This was totally uncharacteristic of the pitcher whom I had seen on many occasions doing the correct thing! This had never happened before. Why now? Why does she suddenly do it with an important run on third? Is she sick, or what the hey, is she just human?

We coaches must recognize that our players are just kids. They are subject to emotions, hormones, bodily functions, and personal problems. Each and every one of these things affects everything they do, including driving a car, relating with loved ones, and playing softball. With their complicated lives these days, it is a wonder they are able to play the game as well as they do.

If I appear to have copped out on this one, please note that I have copped out, because there is no obvious answer. I can only suggest that coaches learn to live with these "minor" coaching annoyances and do the best with that which is available. It may simply come down to sitting back and enjoying the show. Perhaps if we downplayed such situations and looked at them as inevitable consequences of having a team, we would be better off.

There will be those who will not accept this, of course. But for them, there will never be tranquility; only frustration in trying to figure out which team will be on the field on any given day.

Chapter 34
HITTING HEAD GAMES

She was all rapt. Choked, as they say. But why?

"Well," said the batter. "The pitcher, Sally Junkballer, had dyed her hair, was wearing sunglasses, and had beaten everybody in the state. Besides, she grunted and yelled when she pitched the ball. She threw her head all around and just generally got my goat. I just hate her!"

Looks that way to me, but why?

"Well," said she. "You don't understand! She keeps beating us, and I just hate her!"

Ever witnessed this scenario to one degree on another? Sure you have, and often. What's the problem? Why can't this "dyed" in the wool pitcher be beaten? Is it an unsolvable mystery or can we find the secret?

Let's see. She dyes her hair a goofy color, and her opponents dwell upon this. She wears sunglasses, eerie ones at that, and no pitcher has ever done this. Wearing sunglasses ain't healthy, line drives and all. But she also makes loony noises and tosses that head of hers around when pitching. All of this just drives batters nuts. Not only that, but she is cocky...oh, so cocky.

Drives batters nuts – hmmm – let's see what lurks in the shadows of the pitching mound. Stands there a not so dumb creature, methinks. Her fast stuff isn't particularly fast, and her ball doesn't have a great deal of movement, but she continues to get batters out. The mystery deepens.

Then our batter sees Dad over there, pacing about like a lunatic, and acting like the mob will wipe him out, eat his children, and burn his house if his daughter strikes out again. Mom frets and becomes busy pretending not to notice the situation.

Our batter says, "Look at the railbirds over there. They keep telling me to get my bat high, my shoulder down, widen my stance, and to get my head in the game. Coach keeps jumping up and down yelling inane instructions, and Sally is standing out there on the mound grinning under her lousy hairdo. There is a bunch of people watching, and three runners are getting set to go on the pitch. You ordain there is some sort of mystery? If I didn't have to show respect to my elders, I'd call you a moron."

Fact is, little batter, you don't have the problems you are imagining. There are some things you must understand if you are to become a true hitter. They are fundamental things, simple really, but very basic and necessary.

You have been trained in practice to hit the ball down and hard. Nothing has changed between practice and this day, this hour, or this time at bat. The situation of a runner on third, no runner on base, first inning, seventh inning, extra innings, or bases loaded, does not change your function. Your job remains the same.

Least of all should you be worrying about Sunglasses Sally, for she is playing a head game, trying to make you forget your mission. If she can make you think about her little idiosyncrasies, she has won the battle before she pitches. You must not allow her to confound you and deny you the opportunity to execute that which you have been trained to do.

You must remember that Sally is just another person throwing the ball towards the plate. Nothing can happen in the game until she does just that. It is her function to do this, and it is your function to hit the ball if it appears in the strike zone. Sally's actions cannot change any of this.

Now, it is important that when you get into the batter's box, you will have already conditioned your mind to be a great hitter. You will be relaxed, determined, and confident in your ability, your training, your teammates, and your coaches. You will look to the field and see holes, not fielders. You will picture a hit going between the outfielders and yourself sliding safely into second base, beating the throw by an eyelash.

Regarding the pitcher, you must not view her as a person, but as a thing that will throw a ball, much like a pitching machine. Your concentration will be only upon the ball, not the pitcher, her hair, her grunt, or her motion. There will be no hatred in your mind, only the feeling of success. Determination is your ally.

This belief in oneself must be present if one is to be a great hitter. Confidence, not cockiness, is a must.

Well, now, maybe some cockiness is in order. Not because you are cocky, but because you know how to play games, too.

Now the tables are turned. Now the pitcher's mind begins to reel. Your confidence might be construed as cockiness by the pitcher. She has seen you practicing before the game, working hard, hitting line drives. She has seen you in the on-deck circle, swinging confidently. She noted your confidant approach to the plate, uniform worn smartly; head held high, and a gleam in your eyes. Now the head game has changed partners, and the pitcher has begun to worry about you.

Through practice, you have learned about a switch in your head. This switch can be turned on and off. It controls your concentration. If the switch is on, all sorts of menacing things come bouncing into one's head. But if you can turn the switch off, then all the ravings by the coach, the advice of the railbirds, Dad's pacing, Mom's fretting, can be shut out of the mind.

By doing these things, the pendulum of successful hitting will swing your way. You can win the hitting head game, but that game has no score and no trophy. You win by knowing that you always play it to your advantage.

SMITTY SAYS:

Coaches, keep this little scenario in mind the next time some Sally Junkballer has your batters quaking in their spikes. Convey these wise words of wisdom to your batters, and the tides will likely turn.

Chapter 35
MR. FEAR

Mr. Fear approaches the softball player. He is scary. He says, "You are afraid. You fear two things. You fear being hit by the ball and you fear failure. You are afraid! Do you hear me? Afraid. Ah, ha, ha, ha!"

Yes, kids have these fears and because of them, they tend to have much difficulty with their assigned tasks. Their fears often eliminate any possibility of success. Let's see about a remedy that will make Mr. Fear afraid to come around.

Getting hit by a ball hurts, no question about it. The younger the player, the more it hurts. When hit, older players try to act tough and not cry, but you can see the tears welling up in their eyes when they get bonked.

And there have been some terrible bad hops into faces, arms, legs, ankles, and torsos. All players have experienced these episodes in one form or another and with varying degrees of pain. All have seen others go down, and often. It is frightening to watch and painful to experience.

Good fielding techniques, properly taught and practiced, will eliminate most problems, but not always. You can do everything perfectly, but you have no control over the direction of a bouncing ball, or a wind-blown fly ball. The best we can hope to do is train correctly so that injuries are minimized. When they are not, well, then we have to learn to live with the consequences. The only alternative is to quit the game.

Coaches must caution players that there is no such thing as a routine play. Each one must be handled as expertly as possible. It is Smitty's Law that says: Proper fielding techniques will not only tend to avoid injuries, but will result in outs.

Mr. Fear approaches batters, too, and says, "Look out! She has beaned two people already. You could be next!"

Ah, the dreaded beanball! It could well be that the fear of being hit by a pitched ball is the reason batters take their stances with a high front shoulder. They may subconsciously think this offers some means of protection against a pitch to the head. They could be right.

Then, too, there are the situations where batters are hit just as they commit to a swing. They are at the mercy of the pitch on these occasions, and there is little they can do to avoid taking a hard one. For example, a hard riser, up and in, can be devastating. A player, squaring to bunt, can experience dreadful consequences on these occasions. Pitches that bounce in offer similar predicaments.

Coaches should spend some practice time throwing whiffle balls at batters. Do this from a short distance to minimize reaction time. Teach players to duck down and in, thus protecting the head, knees, and ankles. They should be taught to bring their arms in as they duck in order to avoid blows to elbows, wrists, or the hands. The turn of the backside should be just enough to allow for a glancing blow, minimizing the threat of direct trauma to the spinal cord. This practice teaches batters to "roll with the punch," so to speak, thus softening the hit. Hopefully, if they do take a "shot" it will be in a soft area and not on a joint or other vulnerable spot.

Throw some whiffle balls at batters feet too, so that they will learn to jump out of the way. Even here, a bouncing ball from a flamethrower can hurt. It does pay to practice these things.

Mr. Fear, seeing your efforts, asks, "So, you've practiced and learned how to handle batted balls and beanballs? You are no longer afraid of being hit, eh? That's O.K. I've still got you in my clutches, because you fear failure."

Continuing, he says, "Yes, my dear, since you've been a baby, your parents and coaches have taught you that it is horrible to fail. If you strike out with the bases loaded, you're a bum. You will suffer untold agonies from your loved ones and the coaching staff if you throw a ball away or make an error on a play causing the

---

SMITTY SAYS:

Coached in the proper way, our players will say, "Take a walk, Mr. Fear. I do not fear you!"

team to lose. Yes, you are afraid as you stand in the on-deck circle, awaiting your turn at bat. You hope the batter ahead of you gets a hit so that you won't have to come to bat in a tight situation. When in the field, and the winning run is on third, you hope the ball will be hit to someone else. Yes, you are afraid. Do you hear me? Afraid!"

How do we conquer this kind of fear — this fear of failure? It is a fear ground into players from the moment of their first competition in anything from hopscotch to softball. It is ground into the very being of players by coaches, parents, and spectators. It is the American way. Success or failure. Greatness or you're a turkey.

It may be that this fear of failure is harder to handle than the fear of being hit. In fact, it may be responsible for more losses than any other singular thing. It is the source of tension, indecision, and frustration — all of which will cause failure. So, quite often, player's fears actually materialize.

As a coach, you may not be aware of this fear in your players, but it is there. Great players conquer it, usually on their own, with experience, and maybe with some help from understanding coaches and parents. The lesser sometime have more difficulty.

As players go up in the level of play, the pitching, as well as the defense, gets tougher and tougher. Similarly, hitting gets better and better. But it is only the better players who have beaten Mr. Fear. Success at the plate, on the mound, and in the field becomes more difficult to achieve for lesser players.

Pitchers who excel in high school often fail in college. Pitchers entering college must attempt to imagine the toughest hitter they have ever faced and then imagine nine of them in a college batting order. Scary, no?

Similarly, what goes for a "gapper" home run on a grade school team is often caught by a high school outfielder. A hot grounder in the "hole" is often routinely snared by a college shortstop, and the batter thrown out by a step.

So, for many players, what was once success becomes failure as they rise to higher levels of play, and Mr. Fear faithfully accompanies this progression.

Mr. Fear can be beaten if we coaches will only take a different approach to failure. Instead of treating it as a negative, try treating it as a positive. There is a reason for failure. A strikeout occurs because the batter misses the ball. That is obvious, but why did she strike out? An error occurs because of a breakdown in fundamentals. If we find the reasons for these failures and correct them, our players will fare far better. And, our players must understand that failure is not the end of the world, for we all fail many times in life's ballgame. Coaches must teach this concept if they want success.

Chapter 36
THE MEEK GO HOME

Defense controls offense? Nonsense! The reverse is generally true. A tenacious offense will absolutely dictate its terms to a defense almost every time.

Well, now, what about the dominating pitcher or the junker who throws nothing but magic? Won't they do the dictating when on the mound? Sometimes, but not necessarily.

Indeed, we must give the aspirin tablet thrower her due, and we must praise the junk ball pitcher when her ball is reciting *The Constitution* on the way to the plate. During long days, only voodoo and witchcraft will prevent such persons from enslaving even the mightiest of hitters. But perhaps we can conjure up some sorcery of our own during these times and in those games where the more ordinary, less divine-like hurler is on the hill. I have always advocated an aggressive offense: hit the ball down; hit it hard; run aggressively; steal; slap, push, and drag bunt; force the error; get on base.

Many have advocated an aggressive offense and have emphasized the "on-base average," as being of prime importance in softball. There must be something to it, because teams that employ the tactic are usually quite successful.

While watching recent national tournaments, I have been astounded by the lack of aggressive play. Fine pitchers, some good defense, timely hitting, and some luck brought many of the teams to this event. Stolen bases, squeeze plays, hit and run tactics, going on contact, delayed steals, steals with runners on first and third, taking extra bases on outfield bobbles, and other aggressive softball techniques were notably missing. Although not present on all teams, conservatism was the apparent watchword on most. And for this majority, a grand mistake, for they generally went home early.

Aggressiveness applies to fielders, too. Players must: Go for the ball! Try for the catch! Dive! The ball must be kept in the infield, because the runner on second will score if it gets through to the outfield! The outfielders must stop hits or catch them in the gap, else the runner on first will score! Get the ball! Make that play! Play the game hard and fast. "Aggress" the opponents to death.

Yes, a defense, properly schooled in the art of being aggressive and positioned correctly will allow only perfectly placed hits to fall in. This simply does wonders for a pitcher's ERA and definitely gives a boost to a team's winning percentage. These attributes boost the old team morale, too, since aggressiveness is contagious and binds kids together. It certainly helps get the job done.

Will this defensive aggressiveness result in balls getting by fielders for extra bases on occasion? Certainly. But if correct fielding techniques are taught and there are proper backups, these dangers can be minimized.

By its very nature, aggressiveness demands that players be allowed to make their own decisions when running bases and making defensive plays. Coaches who try to control these actions run the risk of defeating their own goals, which presumably have to do with winning contests.

For example, batter-runners should be allowed to take a peek at a hit ball and make their own decisions as to whether or not to advance. A runner at third must make an instant decision as to whether to go home on a passed ball or a sacrifice fly. Coaches who insist on making these decisions for players lose valuable time in the process, because commands to players must be spoken, heard, and then acted upon. Such coaching instructions pilfer the time that runners simply cannot afford to lose.

By reacting on their own instincts, players will gain time and will tend to be more successful than when being directed. Again, there will be blunders, but what coach has not made mistakes when directing runners?

Stealing comes to mind here. Whereas some catchers are quite good at dealing with theft attempts, such perils should not require runners to remain at an assigned base. Testing the catcher is certainly an option, and might even be successful. It is Smithy's Law that a runner left to die at first base, is a runner left to die.

Coaches who advocate being aggressive must absolutely allow for the inevitable goofs which will occur, namely: base running

SMITTY SAYS:

Players should not just run to bases, they should attack them, all the while planning to attack the next base. On a ground ball, for example, runners often make the assumption that they will be out and they more or less give up. This is a mistake and will definitely not help run production. They should go into bases aggressively with the thought in mind that they will be safe.

mistakes; runners getting doubled off; unsuccessful theft attempts; players being thrown out at the plate; and sundry other misfortunes of war. Players in these cases must never be criticized for being aggressive, even though their actions are sometimes in the ill-advised category. Any such criticism sends a false message to the team and promotes confusion. Rather, high fives should be the proper response when an adverse result occurs because of an aggressive move, even though the move might be a bit "suicidal."

Parents and fans, unaccustomed as they are to aggressive play, usually react in a forlorn manner when this type of play has poor results. They must be schooled in the fine art of playing the game as it should be played — wide open and with wild abandon.

There are myriad of examples where players have made the difference in a game by being aggressive. I recall one game where a player hit a pop-up to a very skilled shortstop. There was no question that the ball would be caught. But there was a question in the mind of the batter, for she hit first base and was going full speed into second just as the ball fell at the shortstop's feet. A sacrifice moved her to third. The team in the field was so completely discombobulated that a suicide squeeze was not even a whisper of a thought. The whisper became a shout as she scored the winning run.

Take it from me, the meek may well inherit the earth, but they will spend precious little time in the winner's circle.

Chapter 37
TRANSLATION FROM ENGLISH TO ENGLISH

Once upon a time in Outer Podunk, a horde of barbarians assaulted a castle. The savages spoke the language of the guard and bade him to lower the bridge. He said he would if only they would spare his life.

Now, the words for "life" and "wife" were almost the same in that ancient tongue, differing only in a slight inflection of the voice. Unfortunately for the sentinel, the attackers confused the terms and he was killed. His spouse, however, lived to a ripe old age.

Clearly, the miscommunication induced a result not entirely to the liking of our unfortunate operative. So, what does this have to do with our game of softball?

Well, let's take a gander at another interplay concerning words. A head coach I know, while working with hitters, continually used the phrase "Keep your hands back." Each time he uttered these apparent words of wisdom his players would make curious faces and glance at each other in a questioning manner.

Finally, I "a-hemed" the head poobah and asked whether I might have a word. He nodded assent most reluctantly, feeling no doubt that I was somehow challenging his metal. I summoned the team to center court and asked, "Do you understand what coach means when he uses the phrase 'hands back?'" Nary a hand went up. Zounds!

Coach explained what he meant and all was well. Think of it! For years this coach had been using a phrase that was not understood by his teams. Think, also, of what must have been countless other words and phrases that perished not unlike the castle guard.

The saga of miscommunication and mumbo-jumbo is responsible for myriad team problems. Every coach must be alert for players who do not understand what is going on or what the coach is trying to convey. Such complications cry out for resolution.

Very young players often have the most trouble understanding coaches, although older ones have this problem, too. It should

SMITTY SAYS:

You can talk all you want about concepts, fundamentals, goals, and all your high desires and ambitions, but if you disregard communication, understandable communication, your sought-after results will fall by the wayside. Say it in English, do it one step at a time, and you will be delighted with the results. You might even have a long career as a guard at the castle.

be a self-evident truth that your players must understand that which you are trying to convey — a nicety commonly forgotten.

For example, you say to a batter and a runner, "Now, we will institute a hit-and-run strategy in this situation in order to put pressure on the opposition."

At age nine, your players will not understand the words, much less the strategy of "hit-and-run." Older players may be in the same boat. I've run into collegiate players who have no idea as to what is involved with this strategy.

Instead, we might say, "Hey, gang, right now I want the player on first to run when the pitcher pitches the ball, and I want the batter to try and hit it on the ground. We call this a 'hit-and-run.' Do you understand?" Simple words, understood simply.

Then there is the example of the fielding drill where we say, "Look the ball in." Now, on the surface this seems simple enough, but what meaning does it have to a young player? She may watch the ball by turning her head, look at it from the bottom of her eye sockets, or not look at it at all. The more she gets "bonked" by grounders that decide to leap up and smite her in the shins, the more she will shy from the desired result. You must explain to her that by looking the ball in she is likely to lessen the likelihood of injury. She may find this to be quite "cool," but will lack the coordination to execute the intended maneuver.

In these cases, it is clear that the mind and the body lack communication. It may be necessary to demonstrate what is required by physically manipulating players through the skills desired. By using this method, understanding will come easier.

Often, understanding is thwarted by the presence of a ball. We can eliminate this impediment by not using one. I use an invisible ball and call it *Mr. Magic Ball*. It is free and you can make as many as you want. Kids can borrow it and keep it. It works wonders. How? Well you can do all your drills without a ball. Yes, every drill you have ever done can be done in this manner. There have been tournaments where umpires would not let kids throw grounders to each other between innings in the interests of saving time (which it doesn't). So, some teams simply pretend they are throwing a ball, fielding it, catching it, and otherwise going through the motions of an infield practice. Outfielders can even practice using Mr. Magic Ball.

Once players get the hang of things, a whiffle ball, rag ball, or sock ball can be introduced, with the real ball coming after they master their skills. If players have trouble with the real ball, go back to square one. It takes a little time, but so what?

MISS (Multiple Instruction Syndrome, Stupid) often comes into play, too. It goes like this: "Okay, pitcher, take the ball; use a cross-seam grip, use your pivot foot to turn; stride with the other foot, but not too far or too short; bring your arm around in a purrrrrfect circle; snap your wrist at the hip; and make a good follow through, Got it?"

"Got it!"

Pitch goes over the screen. Coach gives another series of instructions followed by, "What's wrong with you? Why can't you throw strikes?"

Tearfully, "I don't know."

Ever hear this? Well, MISS is prevalent everywhere, and if you haven't heard it in one form or another, you've been in softball limbo.

The MISS enigma can be alleviated simply going to one-step-at-a-time instruction, using simple language. This is the way we all learned to crawl, walk, tie our shoes, and talk. If you force the issue on a player, continuing to give puzzling instructions, punctuated by large words, the fundamentals of your softball players will head south. Yes, MISS will cause you to miss.

Part Seven:
THE ART
OF COACHING

Chapter 38
WHO'S RUNNING THE ASYLUM?

Before getting started on a bit of philosophy, it must be said that there are human beings out there in the coaching ranks who are doing a great job. Many others could use a bit of improvement. But for any coach there are sundry land mines, pitfalls, and other woes — both on and off the softball field.

As one progresses up the ranks of coaching, the problems multiply, not lessen. To be sure, coaching at each level, from nine-year-old teams to college, has its own set of problems, but it is a certainty that as one progresses in level, the problems multiply exponentially. Frustration is an accompanying condition. In fact, it gets outright maniacal at times. Sometimes the plights are self-imposed, but most are not.

Those who have never been a head coach cannot begin to imagine the problems that migrate through one's mind night and day. If the season is going well, problems are minimized, but still exist. If things are going badly, small problems become huge, and big problems become unbelievably inane.

Head coaches, in general, do not sleep well at night. They wake up, sometimes bolting upright in bed, shouting out instructions or imagining all sorts of things. Three zillion lineups will go through each coach's head before blessed sleep comes. The morning often brings a slow venture from the bed to the bathroom mirror, where dark, baggy eyes gaze back in horror at the image.

Summer coaches have a variety of enigmas, some of which are scheduling, umpires, attitudes, money, transportation, idiotically-run tournaments, unruly fans, in-house administrations, and parents.

High school coaches have scheduling done for them, and in most cases the money is allocated, but they are still hit with the hammer of unsympathetic administrations and the meddling of parents.

Politics! Ugh! It is a noun that plagues us all in the coaching world. To play the mayor's daughter or not, to yell at the school board member's kid or not, etc. You get the point.

College coaches grapple with several "governments." Government number one is the Admissions Office, which normally is very sympathetic and helpful, but very unsympathetic where marginal students are concerned.

Regime number two is the Financial Aid Office (FAO). Members of this post feel that it is their inveterate duty to make life as miserable as possible for coaches. This is not always the case, but even where FAO people are sympathetic, it is their sworn duty to protect governmental collegiate funds to the death. Probably, it is for the good. Were it otherwise, coaches would rule the world.

Next comes the "government" of Administration, which includes the deans, el presidente, the provost, etc. Loyalties here vary. Most are somewhere left of communism and feel athletics are a necessary evil to keep institutions afloat. Some pay lip service to athletics and go about the business of running up educational costs by creating bureaucracies second in complexity only to the federal government. Some take an interest in one or two sports, while a few are reasonably indulgent of athletics.

Number four is the academic monarchy. My in-depth study of this situation has determined that exactly 33 percent of all teachers hate athletics. A like number can take it or leave it. Of the remaining third, 20 percent are for football and nine for basketball, with the rest concentrating on curling, badminton, and rowing. One hundred percent of all teachers in Indiana attend 100 percent of all basketball games and sit in the gymnasiums grading papers in the off-season

---

SMITTY SAYS:

Whatever the problems, if you want to coach, be prepared to deal with them. You must make sure parents and players are aware that you run the asylum and hold the keys. Forget the "minor" complications and give the team your best. That's what you ask of them, isn't it?

Last comes the "government" of Athletic Administration, its staff, and the various coaches. Normally, as one would guess, this group is comprised of individuals who like athletics. The problem is that they all have tunnel vision.

Only the softball coach likes softball. All the other coaches want only to discuss and observe their own particular sport. If a softball coach excitedly shouts to the volleyball coach that a world-class softball player has just signed, the other coach will immediately fill the softball coach in on all the great volleyball players signed or under consideration. The softball coach will be left standing in a condition of incredulity. Further, don't mention a softball score or the other coach will fill you in on an entire season.

The athletic director and staff always have a favorite sport or sports, none of which is softball. You see, softball is a necessary evil, and the only requirement is to pay lip service to the sport. Gender equity prevails.

According to my survey, members of the above "governments," if grouped together, rarely overwhelm the seating capacity at softball games. Other interests prevail.

Then there are the railbirds. They are not a "government," as they do not directly influence teams. This is a special group that migrates from game to game. Congregations abound and constantly second guess coaches regarding lineups, strategy, and who should be playing where, and how much. Advice is generally not lacking, but they are harmless souls.

There also is a pseudo "government" involved. It is called "parents." This regime demands control of all the elements of coaching, but will disappear when challenged or when work is to be done. Of all the coaching problems that one could imagine, this area rates number one. Oh, my.

Kids are different today than they were five or 10 years ago. Most are good kids, but there is a large group that is very different. They have absolutely no sense of humor, feel the world was created strictly for them, and tend toward neurotic behavior. They are not disciplined, and are very intolerant. They will not accept instruction. As inmates, they sometimes run the asylum. I dare say no more.

Chapter 39
THE COYOTE ASKS QUESTIONS

One day whilst admiring the foul lines on a softball field and musing about my past indecorous softball misdeeds, a youthful Chicago area travel team coach, one Ralph J. Wiley, introduced himself. Upon hearing the name, I immediately thought of the cartoon character, Wile E. Coyote, and subsequently often referred to Ralph using that nickname. As I later learned, it was not entirely unbefitting for he was not only a shrewd and astute coach, but he was engaged in the pursuit of Wile E. Coyote's nemesis, the Roadrunner, a crafty and illusive opponent.

Ralph was full of energy, eagerness to learn, and excitement. His future as a coach looked bright. Indeed?

Ralph and I talked of various matters pertaining to softball after which he handed me a short dissertation to read. It was hauntingly precise and set forth the frustrations of many a coach. He consented to putting it in print. Here it is with a couple of minor alterations:

"Over 10 years ago, I made a decision that will affect the rest of my life. It was not the decision to play and win the Illinois lottery, to move to Hollywood and become a star, or to look for Elvis, but to try and make a difference in the lives of young athletes. It was a decision to do something that I feel few people can truly do well, and that is to coach.

"If you were to look up the word 'coach' in the dictionary, I would hope the definition includes the words 'caring,' 'patience,' helpfulness,' and even 'love'. These are things that are needed to be a truly good coach and things I've learned to do since becoming one five years ago.

"Unfortunately, as I continue, it becomes more difficult to be patient, to care, to help, and even to love the young athletes. Why is that? Am I changing? Are the athletes changing? Are the parents or society as a whole changing? These are questions I find myself asking every day. It is very frustrating that I don't know the answers. The only conclusion I have come to is that even though it is becoming harder to coach, I still love it and I want to continue for a long time. Yet, these are questions that bother me greatly.

"Throughout the past five years, I have worked with many young athletes. I can honestly say I have never coached two who had the same personality. I doubt that I will. I don't believe this is an unusual condition. What is puzzling (and this goes back to not understanding certain athletes) is why there is a wide range of difference between them? Let me give an example of two totally different girls playing on the same softball team.

"Julie is an excellent athlete who is admired by her teammates because of her abilities and the effort she puts into playing softball. She is such a good athlete that she rarely has to sit on the bench. Unfortunately, Julie is not considered a 'team player.' Even though she plays the most, she complains that she is not playing the position she wants. She often brings her teammates 'down' because of her unhappiness. She also dislikes several of her teammates and doesn't mind if those girls know it.

"Because of Julie, several unhealthy cliques have formed on the team. Julie is commonly called a 'me' player, only happy when she is doing well and getting her way.

"Becky is Julie's teammate. She is also a good athlete and is respected by her fellow players. She only plays one out of every three games, yet never complains about lack of playing time. When Becky isn't playing, she cheers her teammates on and gives them 100 percent support. When she doesn't do well, she remains cheerful and doesn't drag the team 'down'. She likes her teammates, even though she knows they all play more than she does. She would be defined as a 'team player'.

"Why the difference between the two athletes? Shouldn't Becky have been the one who caused problems? Do coaches understand the mentality of these kinds of players?

"Most coaches dream that they would like a team full of kids like Becky, but they know the world is full of Julie types. But there are 'Jennies', 'Michelles', and 'Erins' too. Personally, I've had a hard time dealing with the 'Julies', but does that make me a bad coach? Do other coaches surround themselves with 'Beckys'?

SMITTY SAYS:

More coaches should be like Ralph, forever seeking to find answers to complicated questions.

"I feel frustrated, too, at the lack of the words 'us', 'we', and 'team'. The young athletes today seem to care only about themselves and their own personal statistics. They don't care about how the team is doing. What does it say about a player who bats .500 but doesn't care about the team? How about the kid who bats .125 and is a team player? Who is to blame? The parents? Professional athletes? Who?

"Recently I had a player ask to go home during a championship game because she felt she wouldn't be playing. Her attitude was saying, 'I couldn't care less about my teammates, because I'm not playing'. As a coach, do you try to understand her feelings or tell her to quit for being selfish?

"Another frustration is the complaining or whining parent. Coaches learn to deal with these people, but how about the members of our team? If Becky begins the season as a 'team' player, but listens to Mom and Dad rip coaches and degrade teammates, what will be her reaction? Who is to blame? The longer I coach, the more I think it is the parents who see themselves on the bench or in the field.

"As I look to my coaching future, I wonder how many of my questions will be answered. Will I see the day when parents will parent and coaches will coach? Will my teams have 'Beckys' or 'Julies'? Will I be able to deal with the wide range of personalities? Will I still care for my athletes, want to help them learn, and have the patience to coach and to love them? Will I really care? I hope so, because I always want to be a coach."

Ever sailed in this boat? Sure you have. The tougher-skinned coaches, or less brilliant, among us stick it out, but the rest go on to other vocations. Many good coaches leave because they are unable to solve 'questions', further shrinking the already small pool of dedicated, conscientious, and efficient mentors.

Ralph, the Coyote, seeks the Roadrunner with his questions. He is unable to solve the mystery. His quarry is too swift, too unpredictable, too fickle. His Roadrunner becomes his Holy Grail of softball, ever seeking, yet never finding. But, like Wile E. Coyote, he will continue his chase and do it with dedication, pride, and love...hopefully.

Chapter 40
COACH, BUTTON IT UP!

There are a couple of points about coaching that need particular emphasis. First is the unrelenting overcoaching which goes on in ball games and the negative effect it has upon players' comprehension of what is expected. The second concerns the "have to" theory of a fundamental, such as hitting.

Whether from the coaching box, the dugout, or the stands, we have all heard it: "Watch the ball. Don't overstride. Level swing, now. Get a hit. We really need a hit, now. Concentrate. Think about what you are doing. Watch the release. Right at the hip. You can do it. The pitcher's no good. You can hit her. She's getting tired. Keep your arm up. Relax." On and on, it goes.

Just imagine what goes on in the mind of a hitter at times like these. It happens even in the on-deck circle as the next player prepares to go to bat. There is constant instruction and pressure, pressure, pressure! It is the eighth wonder of the world that the bat can ever meet up with the ball.

Don't you just love the word "relax" when used as a hitting instruction from coaches? Relaxation to a teenager is lying on the floor in front of the T.V. while eating a box of chips. Although the physical condition of relaxation is important in the fine art of hitting, constantly telling players to relax will not accomplish the intended result.

The human mind simply is not capable of handling a variety of instructions during times of extreme pressure. By engaging in this process of overcoaching, we do more harm than good. Other well-intentioned instructions coming from the stands or from the ever-present railbirds add fuel to the mental jazzercise already taking place in the minds of batters.

Should a hitter happen to be successful, the coaching instructions become even more "illuminating" and word-laden.

"See!" says Coach. "If you do what I tell you, you'll be a good hitter. Keeping that back foot down, swinging level, watching the ball, concentrating…all those things I taught you got us a nice hit. Right?" Right!

Try an experiment. Take one of your players aside. Surround the player with three coaches. Have them all begin talking at the same time. One talks about the weather. The second describes the political situation, and the third discusses a softball theory. Do this for 15 seconds. You will see utter confusion on the face of the player. Ask the player to repeat what was said. You will hear an interesting comment. Doubtful it will have anything to do with any of the subjects.

Hey, coaches! This is exactly what happens in the on-deck circle and in the batter's box. It happens to pitchers too, particularly when they constantly get instructions on pitching fundamentals. The mind is literally going in circles. The more pressurized the situation, the more the circles will spin. Is it any wonder there is failure?

The great lesson here is to do your coaching at practice, or if absolutely necessary, between innings. Practice is the place to get the swing where you want it, the pitching motion fluid as a rill, and the fielding habits in place. The more this is done, the easier it will be for players to perform during games.

Our second concern is the "have to do" syndrome. It is part of the overcoaching affliction and builds whatever pressure is already present to unimaginable proportions, a condition that often befuddles youth.

But assuming a bunt or some other offensive strategy is not called, a batter's job is always the same regardless of the inning or the game situation. That job is simply to hit the ball hard somewhere, preferably on the ground or as a line drive. There is no "have to do."

Players do a pretty good job if left alone on the field, particularly if they have been well-practiced. They really do not need much bench or third base coaching instructions during games.

I recall one college championship game vividly. It was the bottom of the sixth and the bases were loaded with one out. The potential winning run was on third. The infielders had worked hard on their fundamentals. They were ready! But, wait! The coach of the team in the field called time and went out to talk to the infield-

SMITTY SAYS:

As coaches, we often get overenthusiastic in our duties, but we can encourage our players to use that little switch in their head to tune us out while on the playing field. Parents and railbirds will be deemed silent as well. Teach players to concentrate on the matter at hand and forget the outside influences. Tough to do, but it can be done.

ers. He told the shortstop to go for the double play, second to first, if the ball was hit hard at her or to her left. Otherwise she should throw home.

There was a hard ground ball just to the shortstop's right. She had plenty of time to go home, but elected to go to third and the winning run scored. To say that a mistake was made by the player is a bit of an understatement.

But, wait! Was it the player's mistake? No way. Coach messed it up. There is no doubt the shortstop would have made the right play had she been left to her own devices.

How do I know? Well, it was my team.

Does this mean we shouldn't coach during a game? Certainly not! Just be careful when it is done. During the nitty-gritty is not the time. Do it in practice. Otherwise, coach, button it up!

Chapter 41
THE RIGHT TOUCH

The brain and the body are curious objects. Neither can function without the other, although we coaches are wont to think so at times, especially when our players take a course of action that we affectionately describe as "dumb."

Sometimes, the brain wants one thing, but the body does another. Other times, the body requests instructions from the brain, but strange messages are received that cause the body to react in an untoward manner. Garbled messages from and between these two entities can be caused by a number of factors such as fatigue, poor training, and, ugh, drugs.

These brain-body phenomena are ever present in our softball games and practices. We coaches want a certain course of action from our players, but often for the life of us we can't attain that which we seek. Much of it goes back to training.

Let's say we are trying to teach a very young player to look the ball into her glove when she fields a grounder. We'll call her Player. Player is having difficulty and does not understand the concept. She looks at the ball and then her glove, but does not look the ball into the glove as she fields it. Not correct! She is going to get bonked in the face when a grounder eludes the field's smooth surface and leaps erratically upward.

We then stress the concept, so she begins looking at the ball out of the bottom of her eye sockets, alligator style. Or, she turns her head and peers at the ball from the sides of her eyes. This is still not

---

SMITTY SAYS:

In many of these cases, by physically showing Player what to do, so that her body understands what her mind is saying, you will be better able to hone her skills. The right touch will, indeed, assist in the teaching of those skills.

what we want, because we know that injury lurks behind every bad bounce.

The body is simply not understanding the brain's signals, so you try telling her to curl her head in towards her belly button as she fields the ball, all the while saying to herself, "Look it in." Still no luck.

So, we come to the conclusion that our player does not have "good hands." She must be exiled to the outfield where it's less dangerous. This is the common thinking, but it lacks the understanding that outfielders need to learn the same technique. What to do?

There is a little magic that can be employed to teach players softball techniques. That has to do with the "hands-on-one-step-at-a-time" method whereby coaches physically maneuver players though the actions they desire very slowly.

In Player's case, we will actually put our hands on her head and curl it in as she fields an imaginary ball. In other words, you show player what you want by directing her body to take a certain course of action. As a real ball is introduced, the difference will be noticed immediately, because her body will understand what the brain wants.

Now, before we go too far here, understand that putting hands on a player can be misunderstood. Before it is done, have another coach present and explain exactly what you are going to do. This protects both coach and player.

The next step is to gradually roll the ball to the player harder and harder. When she appears to have that down pat, try bouncing a few rubber balls at her and then introduce the hard ball again. Gradually move to the field where she can field some easy grounders. She will be ready to get the hard ones before you know it.

Player also has trouble coming off her back foot when hitting. This is not good, because if she continues to do it, she will not be a very good hitter. We've all heard the coaches yell out, "Weight back! Keep your weight back!"

So, you tell Player to keep her weight back, but she either will not, or can not, do it. You demonstrate, but still no luck. This common hitting problem persists.

Try putting Player in her batting stance. Have her slowly swing an imaginary bat and hold her position at the end of the swing. At this point her rear foot should be pointed at about the pitcher's position, but if it isn't, turn it. Then pull Player back so that her weight is on the ball of her back foot and her front leg is straight. Ask her to hold that position and feel what it's like. Then have her swing the imaginary bat with a good turn and her weight back. Have her go back and forth several times and then introduce a bat. Begin the swing slowly and gradually move up to a full swing. She will get the idea in no time.

There is another aspect to brain-body communication. We know that messages sometimes get befuddled by those things already discussed, but there is another ugly monster that creeps into every coach's methodology. That is the ogre of confusion, or overloading.

Overloading occurs when Player is taught too many things at once, usually in a very quick manner. Confusion is the result. To avoid this danger, each skill must be broken down into parts, and each part must be taught separately until it is completely understood by both brain and body.

For example, let's return to Player fielding a grounder. We all know that a balanced fielding position is of paramount importance to good fielding, but if you try to teach it while you are teaching Player to field the grounder, you will encounter trouble. Once Player understands how to field a grounder, teach her the fielding position that will give her quickness to the ball. You may want to do this first, and that is fine. But do not interchange positioning and fielding at the same time.

Once Player has pretty much been able to handle routine grounders and is able to assume a fielding stance as a matter of routine, she must realize there are many different kinds of ground balls. There are those right at her, hit soft and hard. There are those to her right and left that are also traveling at different speeds, and, of course, she has to handle fly balls, cover bases, and learn about relays, etc. The minutiae of softball are many, but each must be covered one step at a time.

Chapter 42
WHO'S AT FAULT?

Suppose we have a player who drops a fly ball, boots a ground ball, drops a throw, or otherwise does something that is not in the best traditions of softball. Suppose the team just isn't hitting. Suppose the "error bug," heebie-jeebies, jitters, or just plain chaos strikes suddenly during a great game. Or perhaps these misfortunes occur at the onset of the game and remain for the duration. Suppose our pitcher can't find the strike zone, and when she does, the ball meets the opposing bats with tremendous force.

It is Smitty's Law that during these spells, bad things will happen to the outcome of the game, unless, of course, the other team has the same villainous deficiencies.

Let's, examine some of these miserable conditions that seem to crop up at the most inopportune times.

The other team may be so overwhelmingly superior that we have no chance and probably should not be on the field in the first place. It is then that the problems on our miserable team get magnified and we get hammered. Not a fun time.

Once I coached a very powerful youth team way back when. A close friend who had a not-so-powerful team wanted to play a doubleheader. I tried to discourage him, but he persisted.

We won both games by two lopsided scores. My friend wanted another doubleheader the next week, and I thought him to be nuts, crazed or a masochist. He persisted and I agreed. We won all right, but by only one run in each game. Wonder of wonders! His team had improved.

Thinking back, I remember that during the two-game catastrophes that befell his team, my friend was constantly coaching. When we hit our "gappers," he used the opportunity to teach his team all about relays. His shortstop had to field rockets, and his pitcher had to duck after every pitch, but after each inning he was busy explaining what had to be done to overcome their various problems. The "dirty rat" had used our first doubleheader for practice! He used us to show his team what they had to do to be winners. He used the loss, the errors, the strikeouts, and the misplays not as negatives, but as positives to learn by. Then, after the first games and before the next doubleheader, he showed his team more fundamentals and, wonder of wonders, practiced them.

What usually happens after a sound beating? Not the above scenario, but a royal chewing out. After the game the team is called to a huddle, and there they sit through yak, yak, yak, and yak. Don't we realize that the kids know they played poorly, and that after the first few minutes of our crazed "speech" they aren't listening? They don't hear us! We are wasting our breath!

So why do we spend time yelling at the team after a poor performance? Sometimes they need it, for sure. Most of the time they don't. What they need is instruction, not destruction. To be told how bad you are time and time again, told you have no intensity, told you don't have your head in the game, and told that you don't want to win, is to be told nothing at all. You are placing blame and trying to find fault.

You scream at the kids, "What's wrong with you? You didn't come to play! You don't want to win!" More fault finding.

But where does the fault lie? Teams do have bad games. That is a given. We coaches have to recognize and accept that fact, for it will come to pass often. But if a team is in a lousy play routine for any length of time there are reasons for the decay.

We can look to many things, but one of the things that cause teams to play poorly is simply incorrect fundamentals or the inability to execute fundamentals. Many coaches don't know how to correct these situations, so they talk. Talking then replaces teaching and gives rise to Smitty's Law that talking does not win games, but correctly practicing fundamentals will.

There is a reason a player strikes out. Perhaps the opposing pitcher is very, very good. This explains much. But most pitchers can be handled. So, if a player is striking out on a regular basis, it is necessary for the coach to find out why and then correct the problem.

If a team does not hit on a regular basis, there is a reason. Perhaps a hitting coach is needed or perhaps a new hitting coach is needed. A one or two game slump is not cause for worry. Consistent nonperformance is.

Why did the shortstop boot the ball in a game? There is a reason that could be explained by a fundamental flaw or simply a bad hop. Why did the pitcher's control suddenly go ape? The reason could be she has a blister or has developed a flaw in her delivery. Why can't we bunt? The reason can probably be found in the lack of practice dictionary. Why does a nine-year-old girl consistently drop fly balls? The reason is that she was never shown how to catch one or the art was never practiced. So, who's at fault?

Why is it that we have practiced a particular play on a regular basis, and yet, when we get into the game, we louse it up? Probably the team is either uptight or the fundamentals of the play were practiced incorrectly. It could be simply a matter of a human paradox.

Why is a team uptight, nervous, scared, or otherwise mentally unprepared to play? The word "unprepared" says it all. Quite often the fault lies with the coach.

Going back to the skill of our opponent, we might witness a great catch of our batter's gapper in left-center field. We will be disappointed, because it would be neat to have that player frolicking on second base. But, is there fault? Can we say we aren't hitting? No way! Fault is not in issue here, for our batter did her job, and so did a great fielder. Instead of laying blame, maybe the fielder should get high fives.

We know that coaching deficiencies are rampant in today's world. Whatever the expertise of the coach, that person cannot know it all. Even if there are qualified assistants, all will not always be perfect. Misfortune will occur in spite of the very best efforts and intentions. Laying blame is moot in these cases, and we coaches should look elsewhere for answers.

SMITTY SAYS:

Mirrors are great for reflecting. Try looking into one when things are looking bleak. Sometimes we can recognize the team's shortcomings in the reflection.

Chapter 43
THE PICKLE POT

Okay. Runners on first and third. A definite steal situation looms. Could be a single steal or a double. Could be a delay. How do we defend it? Easy question. Tough to answer.

Before there can be an answer, several questions come to mind. What's the score? How many outs? How old is your team? What is the athletic ability of your pitcher? Does your catcher have a good arm? Have you scouted the opposition to know what they do in these situations? Is the opposition known as a running team? Are you playing the All-American All Stars or Little Rabbits of the Hobbit? What is the apparent speed of each runner? My, my, the list is long.

Well, what defense do we use? Easy for you to ask. Tough for me to answer, as there are no Smitty's Laws to govern each dilemma. The first and third situation is a pickle of enormous proportions.

Some standard, but not all-inclusive defenses include: a punt (a common maneuver designed to surrender second base); throwing through to second base, take the out, and try for the runner going home; faking to second and throwing to third; throwing to a second base cutoff; throwing to a shortstop cutoff; faking to third and throwing to second; faking to third, faking to second, and throwing to third; throwing right back to the pitcher; working out some kind of trick play; and other variations.

But now we interject the delay "steal" from first to second. The first base runner dances to second or runs half way and stops, all the while attempting to get in a rundown so the third base runner can score.

Let's have a little test. Coach, what do you do in each of the following?

1. Bottom of the seventh. Score is tied at zero and there is no count on the batter. There is a rabbit on third and a turtle

on first. What is the defense if the team batting is known to delay, or is known to run a straight steal, or you are working in the blind?

2. Same as above except the game is in the first inning, and there is a good pitcher on the mound. It's the first inning and the pitcher is so-so, or in either case the game is in the fifth inning

3. Same as item 2, but you have either a good hitting team or a lousy one.

4. Bottom of the seventh and you are up one run, three runs, seven runs.

5. It's the fifth inning and you are down one run, three runs, or seven runs.

6. Same as 1 and 2, but a turtle is on third and a rabbit on first.

7. Same as in all of the above except you are faced with two rabbits, two turtles, or a rabbit on third and a medium speed runner on first.

8. All of the above, except your catcher has no arm, a fair arm, a great arm, no game sense, some game sense or great game sense.

9. All of the above except your shortstop is lousy, so-so, or great.

10. All of the above, except your team is inexperienced, pretty good, or great.

Confused? No kidding. You get the picture, but the problems you are going to encounter are magnified by our old friend time. You do not have much time to confer with coaches, since your pitcher must serve up the old pill within 20 seconds. Ready? Go. But, wait!

You can ask for time and talk it over with the team. Correct, but that means you have used one time-out, and the opposition gets a clue that it is facing a team not up on its fundamentals. Further, are you going to call time each time it happens?

What happens if your play doesn't work, the run scores, the first base runner ends up on third, and the next player walks?

SMITTY SAYS:

Try to keep yourself out of the pot with good coaching fundamentals. That should save you.

Can't call time again unless you want to relieve your pitcher. My, things do get out of hand when we are not prepared.

Now, the secret. The best first and third defense, or any defense for that matter, is game sense and practice. Period. No, exclamation point! You can have all the trick plays in the world, but unless these two factors are present, your chances for successful defense are minimized. Game sense is inherited and cannot be taught. Practice is not inherited and must be implemented. Practice will not substitute for game sense, but it will definitely be an important factor in the outcome of the game.

Remember, if the game is an important one, and if you make the wrong decision and the pickle goes to pot, you will have to face the various chefs in the kitchen who believe they can cook better than you. This assemblage consists of an angry mob of parents, railbird, and fans.

After the game that sported the pickle and cost you the winning run, the other cooks will go to the parking lot and grouse while you have your postgame meeting. When you approach, the parents will instantly spirit their kids away, your assistant coaches will avoid you, and the railbirds will promptly head for the next game. You will be left standing alone. Incidentally, if you make the right call and it turns out badly, the cooks will say you put the pickle in the wrong pot. If things went right, there will be rejoicing.

Chapter 44
THE LEARNING TREE

The human brain is the world's finest computer. It usually has unlimited memory, can be programmed over and over, operates at light speed, and it has a built-in operating system that ceases to behave only when its vital functions are somehow disrupted, usually by outside forces. The software is awesome, and the system operates without batteries or outside power. It needs only the proper fuel to function, which in most cases consists of well balanced meals, plus water.

Given a more or less "normal" brain, a person can learn almost anything, and as they say, but have never proven, it never forgets. Outside or inside forces, however, can alter this function.

Concerning softball, the brain is more than willing to learn, and then to authorize the utilization of that learning in the playing of the game. But the brain must be taught correctly so that muscle processes can proceed with their roles. If there is improper learning, the gray matter will eventually tell the rest of the body that this game is for the birds, and we should go on to something else.

Teaching the young and budding brain to play the game is a real challenge. Most important, it must be a pleasant and gratifying experience. If young players get no enjoyment from an activity, they will accept the brain's recommendations and go on to other pursuits. The lack of enjoyment is one of the things most responsible for kids quitting the game, more so even than the lack of talent.

Now, young minds are little sponges. They sincerely want to learn. If they are being taught something they perceive is good and useful, they will continue to want to learn. In fact, they will demand more information. Coaches must appreciate these phenomena and constantly continue to enhance their own education so that their tutoring will be correct.

Discipline is the next item of importance. Youngsters sincerely want and need discipline. They actually yearn for it, and when not received, something frightful often occurs in the form of anti-social behavior. They want this discipline, but they want it to be fairly administered.

Given fun, proper instruction, and discipline, most kids will rise to the challenge and reward their coaches with outstanding performances. But just how do we go about all this?

I have already espoused that yelling is of little value. It often takes the place of instruction, simply because coaches do not know how or what to instruct. Yelling somehow is supposed to replace knowledgeable and useful training.

Getting hit by a hard ball hurts, in case you haven't noticed. The younger the player, the more it hurts. It just ain't fun. Maybe players should use whiffle balls, rubber balls, or sock balls until they learn how to defend themselves. But then, this isn't tradition is it? We must play with a hard, 12-inch ball. That's the way it has always been done. What wisdom!

Expect your players to be errorless and to not make mistakes, eh? Seems like this is a philosophy employed by many gurus of the game. Believe it or not, players will, indeed, make errors and mental mistakes — even well-practiced players. These "miscreants" must be taught that it is not the mistake that matters, it is how we handle it and then try to prevent it in the future.

Do we return to the bench in shame after a boo-boo, or do we find out what caused it and make corrections? The answer should be obvious. The same is true with mental mistakes. Players must be guided logically through the steps of the play they blew and shown how to remedy the situation in the future.

Age is a factor when enjoyment and instruction are our objectives. Short practices are recommended for very young players, simply because they have an extremely short attention span. For players seven to about 12, depending upon individual maturity, one-hour practices are very good. Frequent breaks should be included. Much over two hours is about the limit for any age. Practice beyond that becomes boring, redundant, and I believe, useless.

Intensive, short practices are very good. Frequent mini-practices involving only a few players, and lasting about half an

SMITTY SAYS:

Players must learn why they won or lost, and which fundamentals were responsible. Then, the game takes on a new meaning. Together with discipline and learning, fun and enjoyment become an integral part of the game. These are the real branches of the learning tree.

hour are quite productive for learning particular fundamentals.

Very young players often do not understand what is being taught, either because the language is too complicated or the skill required is lacking. In these cases, coaches should break down the fundamental into its most primitive parts and proceed slowly. In explaining concepts, try not to use large words. Keep it simple.

Discipline is the nucleus of any successful team. Dictator-style discipline is not required, but kids must learn exactly what coach wants and expects in terms of behavior. It is equally important that any sanctions must be imposed equally and fairly.

No back talk or impudence can ever be allowed. Excuses and the "I can't do it that way" syndrome cannot be tolerated. Sloppy dress equals sloppy play, and this in turn means disaster on the field.

The younger the player, the less emphasis there should be on winning. Winning is the result of the correct execution of fundamentals. Winning should not be expected if fundamentals are not taught, learned, and practiced. Winning and losing are words that should not be spoken to young players, including those as old as 16. Winning is simply not crucial. The learning and execution of fundamentals is. Period!

Athletes these days have the perception that the world hates them when they lose and loves them when they win. They simply do not understand that a win or loss has little meaning outside their immediate sphere of influence, which is usually very small, indeed. The people driving by the ballpark do not care about the game result. It is only the people immediately associated with the team that care, and then only for just a little while. The joy and/or pain pass quickly. In case you doubt this pearl of wisdom, ask the next sports-minded person you meet what two teams were in-volved in the last World Series. Most will be hard-pressed to an-swer.

Chapter 45
DEPTH IS NOT JUST FOR WATER

You've heard it. Sure you have. "The playoffs are approaching, and we are beat up. Lost the shortstop and our ace pitcher has a sore arm. Don't know how we will ever survive. Woe is us."

We, who have coached before, are painfully aware of the above scenario. But did we learn anything by it? Are we in a position to survive those injuries? Can we win the battle with what healthy troops are left as the playoffs approach?

When crunch time comes, a team that is having problems with personnel, whether through injury, illness, or disposition, is generally not in the best of positions. As adversity mounts, losses increase, and the coach feels the brunt of the team's overall unhappiness. Then the bombardment of criticism from railbirds and parents begins from a distance in the parking lot, but advances steadily, gradually growing more intense as the season progresses and the problems increase.

To fix the battlefield, a little foresight is in order. We will mine the parking lot with depth charges to rid ourselves of the unsolicited amateur advice. That'll fix one of our problems. And then, perhaps the most effective maneuver will be to prepare our players to counter any adversity, and we will fix all problems before they come to pass.

First off, it is a fact that injuries and illness do have a price, and the impact is usually quite high if our key players are involved. We have all lost a valuable pitcher or positional player. It is always devastating. It hurts! But with a bit of anticipation, we can shore up our defenses for these eventualities and soften the blow a bit.

Should there be only one pitcher on the team, the coach needs to develop another. This entails some work and some frightful moments as the new pitcher is thrown into battle against foes that could easily be handled by the ace. Yes, losses will result along the way, but if the coach stays with the neophyte pitcher, marvelous things will happen. Not only will pitching gain depth , but your ace will get some needed rest. Nice, at times, during the long, hot seasons, no? Why, we might even prevent some muscle, tendon, or skeletal injury.

It is simply unbelievable that coaches are not aware of the fact that they might need replacements at some point in the season. Can it be that the desire to win outweighs the necessity to develop depth, and therefore only the best nine are played in each and every game? The answer to this is usually in the affirmative.

You can see it over and over. One person pitching both ends of a double header in cold, rainy, and hot weather...the same short-stop and catcher, as well. Where are the relief pitchers? Where is the effort to develop them? Why is no one else tried at shortstop? How come the same people are always in the outfield, no matter the importance of the game, no matter the score? How come?

But coach complains, "I don't have anybody else and those on the bench are incompetent!"

Hogwash and balderdash! If you are a high school coach, have you worked with the summer programs and developed pitchers and other players, or do you wait for the good tooth fairy to put together your team?

If you are a summer team coach, have you tried to find a pitch-ing coach or attempted to work with your kids in the offseason? Have you made some effort to attend clinics, go to higher level games, watch softball videos, or read some of the fine books on the subject of softball?

Whatever your level of competition, have you tried intensely working with the "incompetents"? Have you practiced and played kids in various positions to see what they can do? A shortstop might make a great catcher or vice versa. You never know until you try. But many of us simply make a subjective judgment as to where a kid should play and that's the end of that.

Take a good look in the mirror. Are you really giving your best to your team or are you finding excuses for your failure? Has the team bombed because you failed to do something that could have prevented the catastrophe?

Unfortunately, the desire to win kills all evidence of sanity. Only 13 players are selected on the theory that if there are more on

SMITTY SAYS:

Have faith. Grit your teeth. Suffer through the tough mistakes that are bound to occur while increasing the depth of your team. The rewards will be enormous. That is a guarantee. Depth is a noun dedicated not only to water, but to success as well.

the team, there will be unhappiness. The best nine play most games. Then when disaster strikes the coach bemoans the fact that the team has been smitten by the softball god of losing, commonly known as Your Faultus.

Strange that this Grecian/Roman deity has suddenly risen to smite our powerful group of warriors. It cannot be that I, the powerful, the mighty, the perfect one, the coach, have failed at some point to provide direction, to teach, to prepare for the unexpected. On no, it was not I. It was Your Faultus, the god of unforgiving disaster of losing, who has caused our quandary. Fortunate for Rome that it had no such enemy, else it would not have lasted those long centuries.

So, we can hope for the best and not develop that which might save us in the long, hard-fought, injury-ridden season — that thing called depth. Or, we can work with our entire team, even playing the "misfits," the grunts, the spastics, and the incompetents, fully aware that losses will result.

You see, I feel strongly that if you plan to be successful, the bench is crucial to achieving that goal. The losses suffered will be the strength of your team because the confidence and experience gained will pay off handsomely in the long run. When the chips are down, your entire team will come through like the champions you have prepared them to be.

While it is very true that a team can have a disastrous number of key injuries, the statement that "We had a lousy season because we were young and injured" is a copout in most cases. It is simply that the team was not prepared.

Chapter 46
SHAKESPEARE, MACBETH, AND WITCH'S BREW

After every season we coaches sit around dreaming of next season. We must do better, as we did not reach our goals. There were too many team problems. It if wasn't the girls squabbling, it was the parents griping, and various other quandaries such as vacations and injuries. We were inundated with things we never bargained for during our quest for the Holy Grail. It was a season containing a combination of horrors for inclusion in a witch's brew.

Yes, a witch's brew…a cauldron of evil. It is a phantom thing, many times driving coaches and players away from the game and leaving a terrible sour taste. Let's take a peek at the ingredients.

Double, double, toil, and trouble

Our cauldron of brew begins to fester and is enhanced by our lack of conditioning. No need to train for a season, is there? Fundamentals. What are they? Well, we work on them during practices. What practices? We play a zillion games in a two-month period. When are we going to practice? But we do have a few practices. They start with a chewing out that is a continuation of the scene after the last game we lost. We stretch for a minute, throw for two, get some grounders, then stand around for a long, boring batting practice. Coach and the assistants make speeches. Then we go home. Learned lots today!

Fire burn, and cauldron bubble

Time for the big tournament. Drove all last night to get here. Kids got to bed about midnight. We had a curfew, but some of them could be heard laughing and giggling until very late. Coaches were too tired to get up and tell them to quiet down.

Round about the cauldron go

Up at 7:30 a.m. for the 9:00 game. Oh, don't awaken the kids early and get them moving with exercises and a good breakfast. Let them sleep in. Poor dears, they need the rest. Out with the candy bars and cokes. Leave for the field at 8:15, get some grounders behind second, some flies, and it's game time. Wonder how we got into the losers bracket? Oh, yeah, the umpire cost us the game. We were a better team. Gave it away. Just gave it away. Woe is us, but then if our vigorous pre-game preparation doesn't do it, excuses will.

Next game's at 1:00, so let's get some fast food. Arguments ensue regarding which grease joint will be graced with our presence. Usually hamburgers and fries are on the menu.

The team has internal dissension from this, plus some of the kids aren't playing and the parents are whining, and it's hot, and it looks like rain. Perhaps everyone would be faring better had they eaten something healthy.

And for the evening fare? The choice has already been made. Sausage and cheese pizza all around. No need to watch calories, or worry about fat content. No we deserve a real feast. We know such food is bad for players, hampers athletic performance, yet we allow them such outstanding delicacies. Diet discipline. That's somebody else's problem, isn't it?

In the cauldron boil and bake

Chaos reigns in the next game, but we win 12-11 over LFOP (Little Fillies of the Poor). Coach is happy, though, because we won. Coach is always happy when we win no matter the score. Gloom, depression, and yelling prevail after losses.

Coach says, "We played down to their level. But you guys did real good. No matter that the LFOP pitcher throws junk (in reality, a pitch fed by gravity, zipping in at 38 mph). Now we got to get ready for the big game with the Alaskan Aleuts, just beaten 1-0 in 16 innings by the Fiji Fiddlesticks. Both great teams, but we can beat either of them. They ain't nothin'. Fact that they got a

---

SMITTY SAYS:

Even if you have been a successful coach, there might be a smidgen of the evil brew in your being, requiring that you imbibe in at least a sip of the antidote. Who knows what plague will be dispersed and what plunder awaits?

flamethrower, a great defense, can hit like demons, and are fundamentally sound, is of little consequence to us. We can beat them."

Like a hell-broth boil and bubble

The players are thankful that coach has reminded us how important this next game is, and what they have to do to win it. There's a couple of hours between games, and this was a nice way to spend the time, here under this tree, lying down, half awake, listening to coach. Could have practiced a bit, honed up on our skills, but the players needed their rest to make up for what they didn't get last night. Yep, we are ready to go. I mean reaaaaady!

For a charm of pow'rful trouble

"Gave another one away!"

Yeah? What happened? What was the score?

"Six to zip, but we had them on the ropes. They were lucky. All the breaks went their way, and the umps were terrible. Even though we had three runners cut down at the plate, didn't bunt, didn't steal, didn't do much of anything, I was perfect in the coaching department. Too bad the team wasn't."

Witch's brew…a cauldron full of good intentions and bad ingredients…a brew of failure. The antidote? Simple: education; a willingness to learn; acceptance of criticism; a desire to experiment; and an effort to impart knowledge to others in a meaningful way, with enthusiasm, joy, and a love of the game. Learning, of course, means that somehow we coaches must be educated.

There are many coaches who have paid attention to fundamentals and have shunned the witch's brew. If you keep winning tournaments and get a shot at an occasional national tournament, then perhaps you should continue in your ways. If not, then perhaps you might want to get an antidote to thwart the brew you have been drinking.

Chapter 47
THE YELL, YOU SAY!

I know I've said it before, but I going to say it again, only this time in a chapter dedicated to the subject: I am constantly amazed at coaches who yell, and yell, and yell at players. The yelling goes on, but teaching takes a back seat. I wonder what it is with such coaches, knowing full well that I have done my share of yelling in the past. But, I'm learning.

Once during a game, I watched a team play a pretty good game, but they lost. I commented in passing to the losing coach that his team played well, and it was a great game. Too bad they had to lose.

The coach said, "Well, you may feel that way, but they made me look bad, and I am not going to stand for that."

Amazed, I noted that I really didn't think so; that they made him and themselves look quite good; that it was a great game between two evenly matched teams; and that it was a joy to watch.

"I guess you don't understand," said the hockey puck. "You see, we lost."

With that the coach doggedly walked toward the team meeting and began a one-hour harangue, captioned: "You were terrible."

Well! I wondered why this person was bothering to coach. It was a true mystery, but not one that is so "rare as a sunny day in June." In fact, too many coaches appear to be in the game for the wrong reason. And it's not just softball. It is universal in sports. It is egotism at its very zenith.

In another game I chanced to watch, a softball Einstein, posing as a coach, took 15 seconds during the first inning to alienate the entire crowd. The yelling began the moment the game started and continued throughout the contest. The players could do nothing right. It was difficult for me to believe that the parents did not revolt and empower a new emperor.

About the fifth inning, the right fielder made a mistake. Woe to her! The berating began as she approached the infield after the final out of the inning. It was not a mere chewing out. It was a scream session, with a few spicy words thrown in. It was an embarrassment that was heard three diamonds away. Yes, a new Nero was required, but unfortunately was not crowned by the parents.

Curious, but seldom do these coaches ever show their "recalcitrant" players how to correct their mistakes. "Beration, if I may coin a word, replaces any semblance of teaching.

My favorite example, which we have all seen in many forms during our softball watching careers, is the little girl, perhaps eight years old, who drops what would be a routine fly ball for a seasoned player. The team on offense, especially the parents, cheers as if some great circumstance of monumental and earthshaking consequence had occurred. Kudos are heaped upon the batter in the form of "way to go Munchkin," as if she had struck a mighty blow between the outfielders. Munchkin is made the hero; the eight-year old, the goat.

So, in comes the rogue from the field. Frustrated, embarrassed, demeaned, and ticked. The "goat's" coach yells, "What's wrong with you? Why did you drop the ball? Get your head in the game!" Coaches, parents, fans, and players, I want to know: How many times have you heard these stimulating expressions of guidance and encouragement?

Well, of course, it's not over, is it? Our "goat" is ignored and scorned. Coach's back is turned in disgust, and there is tension in the air. The other little girls look away, imitating their coach. The girl's parents try to disappear in the stands, their flimsy excuses as to why their child dropped the ball having fallen on deaf ears.

Will anyone take the girl aside and show her the proper way to catch a ball, and then practice the art with her? No, better to yell at her, ignore her, and let her continue in her "ill gotten" ways.

All that aside, what does the yelling do? It takes the coach's mind out of the game, for one thing. It takes the collective minds of the team out of the game, for another. It cannot but have an unwholesome effect upon the umpires and the other team. Finally, it causes a fear of reprisal should there be another mistake, for team

> **SMITTY SAYS:**
>
> *To be better coaches, and better people in general, we all need to reflect from time to time on our behaviors. We all make mistakes, but the biggest mistake of all is not correcting the error of our ways.*

members are never sure as to what exactly constitutes a minor mistake as opposed to a "grievous" error that will set the coach off.

But haven't we all gone ballistic at some point? Oh, yes we have, and on more than one occasion. Some of us have done so internally, but many externally. Sometimes it is the result of frustration, fatigue, overwork, injuries, home life, other misfortunes of war, or life in general. Sometimes, we just let it all out, and unfortunately, it is usually at the worst possible moment and vented against a player who has erred in an almost happenstance way.

On the other hand, at times teams and individual players need to be scolded for behavior or inadequacies on the field of play. Teams expect it when deserved. Even then, most teams know they deserve a dressing down, so it is really not necessary to yell at them. Common sense should prevail, but sometimes that inner voice screams, no, gosh dag nab it, they are really going to get it, and the screaming begins.

These characteristics are human and will never disappear. Even good coaches on some occasions will vent their frustrations in various ways, and yelling is one of them.

What is of concern are the maniacs who are constant screamers, belittlers, and naggers...the Negativists.

The Negativists...those that do not teach...those that do not learn...those that believe all players are divined by the deity of softball to play as gods play, without fault, without practice, and without proper instruction. Those of the negative persuasion believe that all wins, no matter how gruesome, are good. They go to the parking lot or bars to brag how their genius resulted in a great win over Little Kiddies of the Poor from Nowheresville. They believe they are the sole reason for the win. They believe the team members are responsible for losses; that players are solely to blame; that umpires, the field, or lady luck are the cause of any misfortunes that occur. At no time in the history of their coaching careers do Negativists look in the mirror and question whether it is they who are the reason for their teams' failure. And often in their judgment of others, it's like the pot calling the kettle black. "I can't stand those people. They are jerks, morons, nincompoops, and are otherwise incompetent.

And I say, "The yell, you say!"

Chapter 48
MAKING A LIST AND CHECKING IT TWICE

Enough of the banter, quips, and small talk. Time to get to work and get the fundamentals of the softball game down pat. We must shore up the "D" to compliment our awesome "O". How? First make a checklist of things you can do to make significant improvement in your team's skills. My list follows. You may want to add some, but it's fairly complete. Remember, in order to build depth, all members of the team should participate in most drills.

1. **Run downs**. Runners caught between bases are free outs. They are a gift from the enemy. We must not return the gift by allowing an escape. Be sure to wear helmets if using real balls. This drill is a super conditioner.

2. **Defending first and third situations**. Include signals and various game situations. Practice determining the speed of the runners. Be sure to include delays as well as straight steals, hit-and-run and bunt-and-run plays, and suicide squeezes. These are common situations during games and must be practiced hard and often!

3. **Holding runners at second and third**. Infielders should drill extensively on this facet. If efficiently done, an opponent's run production will be held captive.

4. **Defending steals**. Who covers second base? Third? And in what situations? Running teams will put our defense to the test, and we must be prepared for them.

SMITTY SAYS:

Writing down your own list is a wonderful way to look objectively at the strengths and weaknesses of your team, as well as your coaching style.

5. **Defending the various bunts, including: left and right drag, sacrifice, safety and suicide squeeze, push, and the lefty slap.** Each type of bunt demands subtle defenses and strategy. Coach must always be on top of the game situation, for decisions here will materially affect the game.

6. **General defense for pitchers, including grounders, line drives, coverage, backups, and bunts.** Pitchers are notorious for lousy fielding. When this aspect is ignored, teams will pay a price.

7. **Double plays, including positioning before the pitch, pivots, footwork, various types of throws and game situations.** Second-to-first double plays are defensive gems and can obliterate a rally.

8. **The ready position for all fielders is a must drill.** Check weight distribution, first move to the ball, glove position, and general stance.

9. **Run-through throws, backhand flip, tosses, pivot throws, and power throws are used over and over during games and must be practiced at length.** All are prerequisites for top-notch fielders.

10. **Charging the ball in various game situations and from different angles.** (Items 9 and 10 can be combined to obtain maximum efficiency in getting rid of the ball.)

11. **Drop and jab steps.** Great fielders use these moves to quickly reach batted balls. Properly taught and executed by all fielders, and assuming they are placed correctly in the field, only perfectly hit balls will fall in for hits.

12. **Get the ball, then make the play.** A fielder is helpless to do anything unless she has the ball in her possession. Often, however, players are so anxious about making a play that they will look up just prior to fielding the ball, resulting in an error. There must be a conscious effort, ingrained by continuous practice, to field the ball first, then make a play.

13. **Mental preparation, both pre-game and during competition, must be a subject of lectures before and during each season.** Teach players how to focus on the task at hand and to block out unnecessary distractions.

14. **Errors...how to handle them physically and mentally**. More experienced players do fairly well in this department, but even they are sometimes troubled when misfortune strikes. Generally, the younger the player, the more troublesome errors become. Our practices are meant to minimize errors, but they are a part of the game and will forever be around. We need to know how to handle them.

15. **One-handed catches and tags**. This may start a controversy and cause some coaches to go, "Hurrumph, hurrumph, what do you mean?" When a ball is hit directly at a player, by all means, catch it with two hands. But if they must run to get it, then try to catch it one-handed. This gives the fielder more speed and better balance. In tagging, one hand will suffice, albeit the ball may occasionally be dropped. However, the tag will be quicker, with better balance, and will tend to keep the meat hand out of harm's way.

16. **Base coverage on tag and force plays at all bases, including sweep tags and footwork**. The force play, which most often occurs at first base, is common, but surprisingly few players know the footwork and the "first-baseman's-one-handed-stretch" technique when the play is at another base. Drill this at length, coaches.

17. **Backing up plays**. Must I say more about this?

18. **Relays**. Proper relays get runners out or otherwise keep them from advancing.

19. **Cutoffs**. I would like a penny for every cutoff person missed. There'd be enough money to build a "Smithdome." The cutoff person must be hit with a good throw, period.

20. **Calling for fly balls**. Who has priority? Practice here keeps players healthy.

21. **Handling sacrifice fly balls**. Come on now, who works on this diligently?

22. **Deep foul flies with a runner on third or fly balls caught running with the fielder's back to the infield**. Watch it here, coach! Runners will move on your defense.

23. **Handling the sun**. Choose your poison: cover the sun with

the bare hand or with the glove? Whichever, work on this aspect.

24. **Handling fences and other obstacles**. More trips to the trainer, or worse, will be avoided if there are drills handling these "minutiae."

25. **Rounding off fly balls and grounders**. Work here and you will save singles from being turned into doubles, doubles into triples, or worse.

26. **Communication**. Call for the ball. Talk about wind direction, number of outs, where this batter hit last time, speed of runners, game situation, etc. This is the alternative to the enchanting expression: "Hey, batter, batter!"

27. **Catching drills**. Another day, another topic, but work here is essential.

28. **Who controls defensive calls, including pick-off plays?** Coach or player? Make a decision and work on it.

Other items of interest that will effect team performance and should be addressed: be ready for a play after a play; there is no such thing as a routine play; know the rules of obstruction and interference; how do you handle umpires and rude fans; how are appeal plays made; how to give an intentional walk; how to pitch out; and general communication on the bench.

Although the above is not a complete list, it will get you started. This groundwork will cause a coach to become ablaze with pride as the winning percentage soars.

Chapter 49
POTHOLES ALONG THE
COACHING ROAD

Someone once said, "You don't know the problems of a head softball coach until you have personally worn the helmet required of that inscrutable position." This is probably an embellishment of some sort of an ancient Oriental proverb, but it will suffice for our purposes.

In other words, you may think you know all about the schtick, but you can never imagine the difficulties until you have actually experienced the position. This goes for assistant coaches, as well, for they are forever pondering changes they would make, and how things would be much better if they were the head guru. Ha!

Well, what are the problems? It might be easier to list the non-problems. Anyway, perhaps I, being the old, worn-out coach that I am, can fetch some words of wisdom for you who might be thinking of embarking on this new gig, or for those who may be thinking of returning for another year of torture. Coaching is torture for some. They gripe the whole season about how tough it is, but then return to do the same the next year. As Yul Brenner said in *The King and I*, "It is a puzzlement." Well, let's see.

Moving, say, from a high school head coaching position to a head position at a college is a gargantuan step, as is moving from a travel team to a head high school job. Even a jump up or down in club team levels manifests unique problems. Having been a head coach at a particular level will, however, be a big help if one makes a change.

The age group you intend to lead will have a direct effect on the number and type of problems you will encounter. Very young players aim various missile-like problems in your direction at every moment of every practice and game. Few are really serious, but each commands your complete attention. For example, right in the middle of an important moment in the game, your .845 hitter tells you, "Coach! I gotta go!" Well?

Some of the problems common to all age groups include: fund raising (and more fund raising); parents (and more parents); various degrees of competence among assistant coaches (where do you find good ones?); motel reservations (there is never any record of your reservation); room and bed checks (or do you let the kids run wild?); food; transportation; equipment, and who handles it; ice and a medical kit (have you had a first aid course, or do you like lawsuits?); scheduling; hiring umps; handling the finances; railbirds (problems with these second guessers abound); and oh, the list goes on and on. Are you prepared for it?

Now comes your attitude adjustment. Have you coached boys? Well, girls are different, in case you haven't noticed. If you think you can coach them the same way you did the boys, think again.

I can assure you that once you have learned how to coach girls, the rewards will be awesome. They will respond as you never imagined. They are willing to learn, anxious to please, and the attitude problem of "I'm the greatest" is not present, as a rule.

But wait! Aren't there attitude problems with girls? To be sure there are. These problems differ from those with the boys. With boys, exactly at age 13, they turn into a pimple and a hormone. They are thin as a rail or on the heavy side, and believe a beard is their pass to bliss; bliss being that very female on earth will fall in love with them. They never get over this until the age of 55 (or beyond), but only when they are no longer able to hit a 16-inch softball and drink 12 beers.

At precisely the age of 13, girls begin a phenomenal change. No, not necessarily what one thinks, but rather a strange mental metamorphosis. Childlike softball players suddenly change from lovable, delightful, wild-eyed, enthusiastic munchkins into ogres.

The "change" involves the following abrupt tumult: a telephone begins to grow from their ears; parents grow stupid and dimwitted, even "impossible;" boys are discovered; eating and sleeping become a dominant priority; the word "relax" means potato chips and T.V.; staying home becomes an abomination; nothing an adult can say or do makes sense or deserves heeding (sometimes with good reason); teachers and coaches are tolerated, but only tolerated; discipline has the same meaning as a four-letter word; and "I just hate softball because coach yelled at me, and said I was

SMITTY SAYS:

Remember, most problems are self-made and should never occur. Others can be swept away with a little bit of knowledge, patience, and perseverance. Keep your broom handy.

such a lousy hitter that I couldn't hit a bull in the rear with a base fiddle."

Coach! Did you honestly tell her that? Well, be very careful of what you say and how you say it. If you say it in the wrong way, tears may appear. Or you may feel the fury of a protective parent, because what you said may be a bit embellished by the time it reaches home.

And don't think for a minute that girls are not tough. They are tough beyond belief. No wimps here, coach. They'll take to the field with a broken leg and an arm in a cast. Your real problem is making them understand that they cannot play with certain injuries

Be prepared for the results of a loss. No, not the fact that the team lost, but the postgame trauma. After your little talk, everyone will leave you. The kids will drift away. Parents who were smiling and happy when you beat Small Sisters of the Impoverished are now scowling and scurrying away. Assistant coaches will inch away to their cars, a bit of a not-so-encouraging smile on their faces, hoping you don't have much to say.

It is lonely now, here in the parking lot. There's nary a person to give you solace. Remember, at the top, you are at the end of the line, the terminal, and the end of the road. If the team wins, the players get the credit. If it loses, guess who is to blame?

Kids crave discipline, love, fun and learning. Disregard these absolutes and you will suffer great indignities forcing you into the belief that coaching is for the birds. Give them these things, and they will come knocking on your door next year. That is your greatest reward, and the true meaning of a successful season.

These are some of the potholes on the road to softball bliss. A few are vast chasms, but most are but a dimple, made large in the imagination only.

Chapter 50
CHECK IT OUT

The "off" season comes to all coaches, players, and, ugh, parents. It is considered a down time by many, a dull time, a time to sit and pout, worry and fret, stew and remember. But need it be this way? Can we do something about those dreaded errors, strikeouts, and base running goofs? Well, get your check list ready, coaches. Now is the time to look for weaknesses in your squad and prepare them for the next season.

Back to fundamentals. They don't just pertain to the way the game is played either. For instance, what is the general physical condition of your team? They should have body fat and weight down to acceptable levels, and be able to run a couple of miles without an oxygen tank. They should have the strength to do basic exercises and sprints without you having to call the paramedics. After all, good conditioning is an absolute must if you plan to be competitive.

Running to first, second, third, and home takes time. Is your squad running correctly? Do they drive their arms, stay low and otherwise use correct technique? You might consider getting a track coach to teach your kids how to run. Running is central to the game of softball.

But it's not just using correct form to run. Runners must run in a straight line when going to first, stealing a base, or going after a ball. Yes, runners often zigzag when stealing or running to first on a grounder. Base coaches can do an invaluable service by taking inventory of the base running orbits and then teaching the kids to run the correct course.

Playing catch is often perceived by players as a necessary evil, especially prior to practice or games. As a result, they often do it in an easygoing and lazy manner. Coaches generally stand by and do nothing during these periods. This is unfortunate, because kids need to have the discipline to throw correctly all the time, or else errors developed in practice will carry over into games. This is not what the doctor ordered, and when losses occur because of errant throws, blame cannot be placed on players. Coaches must bear that onus.

Getting out of the batter's box can be time consuming. Coaches must check things out to see if their kids are getting out of the box quickly and that they have a good start to first base. This is often critical in the grand scheme of things where a couple of steps are the difference between safe and out.

How about fielders? Watch their first move when a ball is hit. It is up? If so, they are losing time. Get that nose down. This is essential.

Do your players know what a run-through is? Do you? It is where a player picks the ball up on the run and while continuing to run, makes a throw. It is a valuable tool, but then you have some coaches who say it is a bad idea to use this technique because it is sheer desperation. Maybe, but only if you want to lose the quick runners. Keep thinking this as the rabbits beat out infield hits. No, any good ball player knows the technique and uses it to good advantage. Those that don't pay the price.

Backhand and overhand flips are important tools, but are often ignored in practices and games. They are useful time and time again and can number over the hundreds in a season. Check these out, coaches.

How about relays? Seems frightfully unfair that you lose games when a fielder misses a cutoff for a game deciding miscue. Unfair? Not really. Just unpracticed. Players caught in rundowns are gifts from the offense. Perhaps some practice time on these little gems would be in order. Should we let a first and third situation control our defense? No way! Find a defense!

SMITTY SAYS:

The checklist is practically endless. Make your own. Get a good softball book, check it out. Check out the items covered. Check out all the aspects of the game. Then, be sure you practice all the check marks and practice them well, for during games, the opposition will be checking to make sure you do.

Kids love to talk, however, on the field, silence is golden, except when communication during a play is required. It is essential that your kids learn this skill. Two outfielders colliding are not a welcome sight, and the circumstance can be avoided if communication is practiced. Further, players who are busily engaged in fielding balls need to hear from their teammates so that the proper play can be made. This aspect of the game must be practiced.

Blocking drills are the prelude to saved games. Catchers having good skills in this department don't just appear on the scene. The are drilled, drilled, and drilled again. Same with pick-off plays. Same with signal calling, tagging, and plate blocking. Your check list must include these items.

Bunting is routinely botched during games, and this result gives rise to many losses. Whether the answer has to do with poor technique or lack of practice is anybody's guess. However, it would appear to be a combination of the two. So, the obvious answer is to get a feasible style and practice it religiously.

The slap is a great offensive weapon. So too is the right- and left-handed drag bunts. But they are routinely ignored in practice and are conspicuous by their absence in games. A great power hitter can get base hits by drag bunting, or at least making the threat apparent so that the infield can't cheat back.

Batting practice is a great thief of practice time. Often it is counterproductive. If a player is swinging incorrectly, you can pitch to her a zillion times and she will never hit in games. Take this to the bank. If she can't hit after listening to your sage advice, find someone else to teach her.

Bet that if you took a poll of your players, they wouldn't know what you were talking about at times. For instance, have your players describe a "hit and run" play, soft hands, intensity, momentum, home cookin', batter in the hole, along with such sage coaching instructions as, "get your head in the game," or the epitome of questions, "What's wrong with you?" Try explaining what you mean when you talk to players. The younger they are, the simpler your instructions must be.

How about pitching? Can your pitcher hit spots, throw different pitches, and field their position? These matters cannot be ignored. If you don't know much about pitching, find someone who does and have them work with your kids. Don't just assume they will get all this on their own.

Chapter 51
ANSWERS FOR WILE E. COYOTE

Well, a few chapters back we saw how Ralph Wiley, also known as the Coyote, was frustrated with youth, their parents, and the problems that seemed to be destroying his love of coaching. I went to press with these thoughts and this brought some response, however scanty in the form of letters and email. Here are three in their pristine state, edited "slightly" for brevity.

Writer One noted that as a parent he had witnessed "coaches who shamelessly promote their favorites (often, but not always, their own children), at the expense of the other kids. At the other extreme, he had squirmed in his seat as some coaches brutally rode their players." He suggested that because of this, kids often cannot develop their potential.

Writer One made note of parents and players who attempted to use politics on coaches and administrators, efforts that are often rewarded to keep the "squeaky wheel" oiled. This, he said, is often "at the expense of other players and parents who quietly sit by and say or do nothing to gain favor."

Along the same lines, Writer Two felt that many players abide by the rules of the coach and/or team, but continue to sit the bench. He noted that "a coach may set standards and require certain activities which are followed by the benchwarmers, only to have their efforts go unnoticed while other players miss practices, show up late, make errors, but continue to play."

Continuing, Writer Two said that "it is my feeling that if a coach truly dedicates himself to giving every girl a shot at starting, works to fully develop each player...establishes fair rules for (those) who play, communicates those rules to the players and their parents, and abides by those rules to the letter, (the coach) will have minimal conflicts with players and parents. The keys are (1) ongoing, effective communication with all concerned, and (2) integrity."

Writer One echoed these thoughts by pointing out that we need "an honest, fearless evaluation of our goals...values of teamwork, discipline, commitment, merit-based decision-making, and sportsmanship." He asks, "Are they worth a loss or two?"

When talking to his players and their parents during pre-season, Writer One explains that he wants to teach the kids the fundamentals and he is not all that concerned about the record. This understanding, he feels, will prevent "a midseason blowup."

Writer Three felt that "many of the problems expressed by the young coach could be avoided if coaches would put some effort into their coaching, particularly their own training (by attending) clinics, (watching) videos, and (reading) books. When is the last time they (the coaches) picked up a book on the psychology of positive coaching, rather than the negative yelling, screaming, ranting and raving that I've seen...(and) why is it that they (the coaches) do not want to better themselves with whatever it takes?"

Echoing the other two writers, Writer Three made note of "the lack of coaching for people who are not first string players...seeing them ignored by the so-called 'good coaches' of today. Perhaps coaches have lost their coaching skills and are afraid to rub shoulders with people who might know a little more. Much of the coaching...still lacks the basic knowledge of fundamentals and how to get (them) across to our players. Maybe we, as parents and coaches, should take a long, hard look at ourselves and see if we are playing the game of life like we are playing the game of softball."

Well! Our young coach shot at players and parents. Our three letter writers point more to the coaches. Let's see if we can't sort some of it out.

We must agree that there are attitude problems with some players and parents, although this may be a prodigious understatement. Many coaches will thunder, and rightly so, that some parents have their own agendas about how things should be and make every effort to make it so. Players often reflect these attitudes. The grief to coaches in some of these circumstances is enormous.

Then, too, there is an incalculable number of players whose family situations cause problems that coaches cannot hope to understand, much less solve.

SMITTY SAYS:

Ponder these questions: Can I do something to become a better coach? Am I teaching the right thing? Have I been unfair with the kids or the parents? Am I the problem?

Athletic ability comes into play. Some kids just ain't got it and others have it in varying degrees. That doesn't mean they can't learn some aspects of the game and be able to contribute to the team. Coaches tend to forget or ignore this condition.

Game sense is inherited. It cannot be taught. You either got it or you ain't, and no amount of coaching will change it. Again, however, coaches must deal with players who lack this savvy, and not blame them too severely when things go wrong.

And, of course, there is always a "team chemistry." Sometimes it is out of sync between the players, between the players and the coach, between the coach and the parents, or all of the above. Good coaches find the right formula, but bad ones suffer the fate of the chemical reaction.

Each coach must keep in mind that he/she is a teacher first and foremost. The teaching profession has its own set of problems, but it is essential that one must take the time to learn what must be taught, and then learn how to teach it.

But, not to worry. Remember that kids want love, discipline, proper instruction, fairness, and fun. In fact, they demand them. If you remember this and listen to the problems of the Coyote and the responses of our three correspondents, your softball seasons will be quite rewarding and most of the questions will disappear.

Smitty's Law decrees that a coach's job is not to win, but to teach. By teaching the fundamentals of the game, and given talent that is more or less equal to one's opponents, winning will be the natural byproduct. How simple. Why can't we coaches learn this? That is the real question.

Part Eight:
SOFTBALL BY SMITTY

Chapter 52
AUGUST LUNACY — AN EDITORIAL

As August arrives each year, most summer softball programs end their season. At least that's what happened in the not so distant past. After a long season, tired and beat-up teams used to look forward to the Amateur Softball Association's (ASA) qualifying tournaments that led to a national championship for the best of the lot. The remainder went home, thankful the season was over, yet looking forward to the next year's engagements.

Times have changed. Teams now have a zillion summer games. In the ASA, these games are followed by metro, state, and regional tournaments. Babe Ruth and Pony Softball have been around for years, but the ASA has been the dominant force.

Now, the upstart AFA and NSA associations have taken hold and each has a national tournament, both different from each other and the ASA in rules and format. Not to be outdone, the ASA formed a Gold Division, comprised of elite teams, and there is a national tournament for that, too. Add the fact that each association has numerous national qualifiers and you have mass hysteria. But this isn't all. The ASA now has a kind of local "national tournament," called Zone Nationals for those teams who did not get to the "national" nationals. Wow! Perhaps there will soon be divisions, such as 1A, 2A, etc., and divisions within divisions. Why, we can have divisional "nationals" for every kid on the block. No problem.

Sounds all too confusing. Guess I am too old, battle-scarred, and cynical, but the way things seem to be going, excellence is in danger of being totally eroded by the contamination of too many associations and national tournaments.

And now as we flit about during the off-season and run into our softball friends, we are inundated with the gloating of coaches, managers, and parents as to their performance at "nationals." A coach will say, "Hey, Smitty, we were third at nationals."

Well, that's great! That's quite an accomplishment, but where were you and what organization were you with?

"Well," says coach, "We knew we wouldn't advance to the ASA nationals, although we entered anyway. So we put in for all the others, knowing that we would advance, since all you have to do in some cases is make a payment in order to qualify or merely win a couple of games against weak teams. That way our kids get the thrill of going to a national tournament."

But doesn't that sort of water things down a bit? If you get knocked out of the ASA tournament, and then qualify in some other upstart national tournament by beating weaker teams or paying money, doesn't that sort of sway the luster, fame, glory, and excitement out of earning your way there by qualifying against great teams? Aren't there six zillion other teams there, including a bevy of "also-rans"?

At this point there are few answers coming from the coach or the nearby parents who have been listening in. It seems to come down to manager, coach, and parent glory more than anything else. The kids, who were utterly exhausted at the end of the regular season, rarely mention "the nationals" when you see them.

So your trip to the nationals included some pool play among the, let's say, 128 teams present. Then you entered a double elimination tournament based upon your pool play standings. You lost the first two games and went home along with 32 other teams. Your coach will say, "We came in 96th. That's not too bad out of the whole country. Just think how many teams there are and we were 96th. Ain't that somethin'? Only cost us 12,000 hard-earned dollars. About 2,000 a game, including pool play. Cheap at half the price." Math always was confusing to me.

Of course, all the teams in the "whole country" didn't enter this tournament, did they? No, these tournaments had the remains of the other tournaments where the teams didn't qualify or where the stronger teams wanted to play due to the weak competition and a better chance to win "nationals."

The point has to do with what we are doing to our kids. Remember when you were involved in "little league" and the governing board did not want to award trophies just to the champions, but to all the little girls so that no one would feel badly? Yes, the losers' entire lives would be ruined if they did not get a trophy. So, now all the softballers will get their participation trophies, which for the most part are constructed mostly of pride.

There are those who would argue that the new organizations give girls more opportunities to play more games at the national level. Can't argue with that! Soon we should reach the epitome of softball, which is that every player will have at one time or another been to "nationals." Such a deal!

The real reason we try to get all these kids to "nationals" is never mentioned. Pride is involved, of course. But it is more about money. Greedy hands see the bucks in national tournaments, qualifiers, and the like. Moreover, the more teams, the merrier, or rather the wealthier the associations become.

The mood today is for all the associations to have as many teams as possible in their respective "national" tournaments. The number is restricted only by the number of available fields, umpires, and support personnel. And heaven forbid that it rains. Then chaos will reign and hundreds, yes hundreds, of thousands of dollars spent will go for naught. Or if play is actually resumed, games will be one hour or less and then at half-witted times sometime after midnight.

Now, just for the record, my summer team went to California recently for a "national" tournament. We were in pool play. There were just under a hundred teams there. We played one pool game a day for three days and then entered a double elimination tournament seeded according to placement in the pool. We were 1-2 in pool play and lost the first two in the tournament. The trip cost roughly $12,000. That averages out to $2,400 per game. And this doesn't even count what the parents spent. Does any of this make sense? Maybe. It was a nice sight-seeing trip for the kids, although where we were playing was not exactly a tourist's delight.

There be will disagreement about all this, but if anyone can rationally justify this madness, I will retire to the fishing pond where sanity is interrupted only by high-speed motorized appliances. August lunacy is here to compliment the regular, unending, zilliongame, softball season, which, in and of itself, is grounds for commitment to a loony bin.

Chapter 53
THE NOSE KNOWS

Once, I was practicing with a kid by the name of Sue, a member of a high-powered 18 and under travel team in the Chicago Area. The nose, of all things, was under discussion; the premise being that a softball player, when running, should start low, and she could do this if she kept her nose down. Further, if the nose stays down while hitting, the batting average is bound to improve.

Sue said, "Yes! The nose knows!"

Very funny, no? But, our players sometimes make good sense, and on these occasions, we should reward them with high fives. When this is done, the player will beam and feel that she has contributed something to the team besides her skill as a player.

So, what's all this nose business, anyway? Well, to digress a bit, if you haven't noticed before now, softball is a game of time without a clock. The game does not end with a buzzer, but there is always the ominous presence of time and its accomplice, speed. Thus, we coaches should always be alert to the fact that it takes time to go hither and yon on the playing field.

Let's digress further and have a review of Mr. Time and the one-tenth of a second sooth. It is Smitty's Law that runners, on average, while at full speed, travel between softball bases (60 feet) in exactly three seconds. This law arose as a result of observations by my personal soothsayer just after observing all the softball players who have ever played and who are now playing. Actually, three seconds are used for easy math calculations, and the only real function of the soothsayer is to advise me when to pull a pitcher.

If the calculations are correct, then runners move at 20 feet per second or two feet in one-tenth of a second. Thus, if an outfielder pumps her arm, not knowing just exactly where to throw a ball, and then throws the ball in an effort to nail a runner, she has lost as much as half a second or more, and thus about 10 feet. Normal people feel that 10 feet in softball is a rather significant distance.

There is another aspect to this. An object moving at 60 mph is traveling at 88 feet per second. Some balls are hit much harder, and this means they will travel farther and faster. Another of Smitty's Laws says that those who are continually unprepared for hard-hit balls will most surely spend time on the pine.

If we work hard on one of the famous and oft-stated theories of playing softball defense — "know ahead of time where to throw the ball if it comes to you" — we will in many cases avoid the embarrassment of a runner sliding in safely. There are other techniques that help, but one of them is starting out low when you begin to go after a ball.

Now, starting out low is not a new concept. It was practiced in the Roman Olympiad many moons ago. It is an effective way of getting from one point to another quickly. None of the great runners then, or today, starts high. They all drive down then come up. Let's translate this to the softball diamond.

Coach, watch the first move of your shortstop's head when a ball is hit to her right or left. Betcha it will be up. This slows her down and her chances of getting to the ball are diminished. If, on the other hand, she drives down like a Roman sprinter, the odds will tilt in her favor.

But, don't just dwell on the shortstop. There are other fielders milling about the diamond. Coaches might take a moment to watch them too, instead of chatting with the railbirds or otherwise wasting valuable practice or pre-game time.

What about the batter's box? Same thing. Swing and drive the nose down as you take off for first base.

Stealing? Same thing.

Going after a kid in a rundown. Yeah!

Tagging a runner? You bet. Get the nose down.

There is another aspect about the batter's box. Barring a walk, hit batter, or dropped third strike, one must make contact with a pitch before running to first base. We coaches all say, "Watch the ball!"

Now, batters watch pitches in many ways, some of which are simply not efficient. If they are closely observed, one will note that they routinely stare through pitches 10 to 20 feet in front of the plate; or they bat with their heads tilted in curious ways; or they look at pitches out of the bottom of their eye sockets; or they follow pitches without turning their heads.

Fielders, too, will look at hit balls in interesting ways as they field them. We are constantly telling our players to look the ball in, but grounders are often muffed and fly balls dropped. Coach then says, "You took your eye off the ball." Maybe, but more likely the player did not curl in as she fielded the grounder or looked up as she attempted to make a catch.

The problem can be solved simply by using the nose. A comforting thought, eh?

Although the eyes are capable of moving disrespectfully in directions other than that which the nose is facing, they generally follow one's snout. Thus, a coach might want to forget the trite phrases about watching the ball in as it is pitched or fielded and simply say, "Take your nose to the ball."

Another little item about the nose. It can be used like a rifle sight. Immediately before making a throw, a fielder can aim her nose at her target. But don't just point it, make sure it's aimed directly at the target and not up. If it's up, throws will generally go high and may be difficult to catch. Better that the nose go down, as throws will then tend to be low. At least low throws can be fielded in contrast to those in orbit. If the nose is level, an accurate throw is in the making.

Yes, the nose knows. You will too, if you use this refinement on teaching technique.

Chapter 54
WHATTA RIDE!

College costs are soaring! They are going up far faster than inflation. Five to 10 percent a year is about average these days. Some private schools are well over $20,000 a year for room, board, tuition, books, and fees. The rest are rapidly approaching that amount. That's no lie.

So how is one to beat the college cost game? Well, most can't, completely. But increasingly many athletes are looking for financial help from schools, and some of that comes in the form of athletic scholarships. Coaches, it will behoove you to be well-versed in the options available for those coveted top-notch players.

For many softballers, the best deal is an academic scholarship. If they work hard in high school, get good grades, and score reasonably well on the ACT or SAT exams, chances are good that there is some academic money available. But if they aren't a rocket scientist, or at least somewhat brainy, what's available?

If the softballers are "poor" or have "need," they may qualify for grant money that can be accompanied by state and/or federal money. This is money that never has to be paid back. What constitutes these situations are concepts that have always confused me and are better left to the various financial aid offices to explain.

Loans, in varying amounts, are usually available to most. What's left besides a few minimal fraternal, local, or institutional scholarships of one kind or another? Athletic scholarships, of course.

Many people think softball scholarships, particularly "full rides," are lying around just waiting to be snapped up by recruits, the only question floating through many softballer's minds being: "Which school will I grace with my outstanding athletic ability?"

Well, let's do some simple math. Let's look at the fictional state of XYZ where there are about 28 colleges offering softball scholarships. If each school, on average, must recruit four players next year, 112 bodies will be required. A ballpark guess would mean abut two thirds (74 plus) of those will come from XYZ and the rest from out of state. There are over 800 high schools in XYZ, and let's say only one-half offer softball. If there are just three softball seniors at each high school who want to go on to play in college, that means there are 1200 potential recruits. Now, not all will go to instate schools, not all will qualify for four-year institutions, and many will go to NCAA Division III schools. So, let's say that just one from each of the 400 high schools wants a softball scholarship at a four-year institution in XYZ.

Our math shows that 400 seniors are looking for over 74 softball positions in our fictional state. But that's not all the bad news for seekers of athletic scholarships. Large softball scholarships are few and far between. "Full rides" are close to zilch.

The so-called "ride" is a bit of an illusion. In terms of percentages, a full athletic scholarship is rarely awarded to a recruit, and then only if she is a very elite player with tremendous skills and injury free. Even then, coaches are reluctant to make such awards for fear that the recruit will not pan out or might receive a career-ending injury.

Remember, too, college coaches have only so much money to award. In NCAA Division I, coaches as of 1998 are allowed only 12 full athletic scholarships, but all colleges do not allow their coaches this many. This means a coach, at most, might be able to award the total sum of 12 times room, board, tuition, fees, and books.

A coach can break the awards down in several ways and give different amounts to many players. For example, a coach might grant "rides" to two pitchers, a shortstop, and a catcher, and then divide up the remaining eight scholarships into varying amounts distributed among perhaps as many as 14 players.

Division II coaches are restricted to eight full rides and Division III has none. NAIA coaches are at the mercy of their individual institutions as to how much they will be able to award.

There is always hope should one not receive a softball scholarship at a four-year institution. There are junior colleges that have excellent programs and whose players are often highly recruited after they obtain their associate degrees. Many offer scholarships too, often full tuition. Then there is the "walk-on" status, where a player tries out, makes a college team, and then hopes for an award after the freshman year.

What constitutes a "ride" is often defined by circumstances and/or the inclination to exaggerate one's status. A player can get a partial athletic scholarship, get some grant or academic money, and maybe some loans, and the total adds up to a "ride." One might live at home, get a scholarship for tuition, and consider it a "ride." A player might be so poor and so destitute that she will receive grants and loans that add up to a "ride."

So, what do the college scouts look for when sizing up a player for a scholarship? Stupid question, maybe. Yes, they all look for the best athlete who has a rocket arm, speed to burn, and who can hit like King Kong.

Next question for college coaches (actually, the first for many) concerns academics. Is the kid a good student? High school and summer coaches often say that she is, but when a definitive answer is sought, the answer sometimes indicates Bs and Cs and low ACT or SAT scores. For many colleges, this is not enough, since they can be at the very minimum or below, NCAA requirements. Moreover, college coaches want players who can maintain their grades during the rigors of a softball season.

Weaker students might do well to go to a junior college or consider not playing at all in college. The college schedule is a grind, tiring, and difficult to handle at times. Pressure placed on athletes is often so intense that academics suffer in the process. On top of this, college professors take no pity on athletes, often piling on the course work irrespective of the softball schedule.

Players must remember that they aren't much good to a softball team if they don't make good grades. This must be an athlete's primary concern if she is to participate on a college softball team.

So, in the end it all boils down to how good the player is, how much she is wanted by a college coach, and the amount she will get to play softball. She can shoot for the sky, and maybe that's okay. But if she misses, don't be afraid to coach your prospective players to accept something less.

Chapter 55
OUCH, IT WAS SO PREVENTABLE

I am sitting her pondering the injuries caused by the rain, cold, and snow here in the North during the dreadful conditions in which we are forced to play the game of softball in March, April, and May. We often sit around and wait for the rain and snow to let up enough so that we can rake the field in hopes that it will be dry enough to at get in at least a couple of innings. The fact that there are a great number of softball teams in the North matters not to the governing bodies. Tradition seems to be the watchword and fall ball out of the question. Advantage South and West?

All that aside, what about the injuries caused by means other than weather? Personally, I would like the majority of my team to be reasonably healthy all season long. As I watch other teams, I sometimes wonder if other coaches feel the same. Clearly they should, but if they do, why aren't steps taken to eliminate preventable injuries? Let's peek at a few examples:

Memory serves that twice in the recent past, the team I was coaching put on suicide squeeze plays. In one game, as soon as the ball was bunted the catcher came out of her position and literally sat on home plate. In the other, she set up six feet down the third base line prior to the ball being fielded. Injuries waiting to happen? You bet! And in both instances, guess what? The catchers were carried off the field.

Who's to blame for the clear catcher interference? Rules state that you cannot obstruct a base without the ball, but umpires will argue that there is no obstruction in cases similar to the above, saying that the catcher was in the act of receiving the throw. Their argument is not without merit in some cases, but if the catcher sets up before the ball is even fielded, where will the fielder throw the ball? To an uncovered home plate? I think not, since the catcher is a more likely focal point.

Of course, coaches on defense will argue that catchers have a right to block the plate. From whence comes that right? Where does it say that the runner has no right of access to home plate? Tradition, most likely. Please don't say that the runner can go around the catcher. Ever hear of the rule preventing such when a fielder is attempting a tag?

Arguably, there should be a rule that absolutely forces anyone covering the base to give at least partial access to that base. This will help avoid injuries, for an advancing runner will invariably go for an open portion of a base rather than make contact with the person covering a base. Will this help prevent collision injuries? You bet. Will it stop all such injuries? Clearly no, since throws will occasionally take the baseman into the runner's base path. Let's hope it will not take an injured player's lawsuit to settle the problem.

Then there is the technique I have seen taught in clinics which champions the second baseman stepping into the base path of a stealing runner. The runner will normally slow down to avoid a collision, but if there is contact, the defense will claim interference by advocating that the baseman was going for the ball. Bush league defense! No other thought comes to mind. An injury waiting to happen? You be the judge.

What about the failure of middle infielders to use the pony hop on a double play. This is a technique that is used to avoid a sliding runner and consists of a vault, or jump, at a time of a throw to first base after a second base force play. Lo, these many years in softball, I have seen precious few pony hops, but a multitude of middle infielders on the ground after a force at second. Some were carried off the field. All should have been capable of running off had their coaches done their job.

The "old college try." What a wonderful thing! Great athletes aspire to this all the time. Running to first base, for example, is an instance when runners give their all. When near their goal, they literally leap at the base. Nice, but an invitation to injury.

First, a leap slows a runner. Secondly, it makes for nice groin pulls, or if the runner is a bit unlucky, her ankle might decide to convolute just as she hits the middle of the base. Perhaps a stutter step prior to reaching the base would put one foot in position to touch the front of the base. This just might relieve us from not only a trip to the trainer's office, but could bring about a favorable decision from the umpire, since the front of the base is somewhat closer to home plate than the middle.

Infielders and catchers have a bad habit of running into obstacles, such as fences, in search of illusive foul balls. Again, the "old college try." Such fielding attempts are not exactly out of the ordinary, so shouldn't we teach the obvious? That is, how to handle obstacles.

Ah, the on-deck circle. Why won't the rules allow an on-deck batter to be in the circle behind the batter, rather than in the circle near the hitter's bench? Sharply hit foul balls lurk with every swing for the visiting team when a right hander is at bat, and vice versa for the home team when lefties are up. Ah, lawsuits in the wings.

Helmet throwers...another abomination. Believe it or not, helmets are made to protect runners as well as batters. Errant throws are far more common than bean balls. So why do coaches allow runners to intentionally remove helmets while running bases, thus exposing not only their precious noggins to poor throws, but also creating a dangerous situation for the defense? Oh, well anything for victory.

These are but a few instances of injuries waiting to happen. There are scores of others. We must be alert for the problems involved. Softball is a great sport, but it can be a dangerous one as well. The success and health of our players depend upon us being aware of these dangers. When we say we had a bad season because of injuries, let it be that these were unavoidable and not something we, as coaches, might have controlled through vigilance.

Injury prevention....just another of the little things that lead to success.

Chapter 56
CRYIN' THE BLUES

Losing coach says, "The Blue cost us the game! The score was 0-0 in the bottom of the seventh, and the umpire made a lousy call at the plate that gave the game to the other team. The Blue blew the call!"

Sounds like this team needs a hitting coach. If they must depend upon an umpire's call to win the game, something is wrong somewhere. Anyhow, it is Smitty's Law that you must score a run to win.

Another losing coach says, "We lost 11-10. The umpires were just terrible and cost us lots of runs."

Looks as if something contributed to the loss other than the umpires' lack of expertise and competence. A pitching and/or fielding coach might be of some assistance along with some practice. Perhaps the team was just tired, overworked, or had some other problems that contributed to the loss.

Yes, umpires do make mistakes, but coaches never do. That could never be one of Smitty's laws, because then several other things would be true, such as: coaches' lineups are always correct; they always put the proper players in the proper positions; they start the right pitcher and pull them out at the correct moment; they direct all runners flawlessly; they know all the rules; and their actions on the field are ideal.

Once, in a tight game, a coach sent a runner on third base home on a wild pitch. The runner was out. Thinking the ump had erred, the coach approached. Now, it was true that the umpire and the coach were old friends and had been in "combat" many, many times, so that this was a familiar happenstance.

Said the coach, "That was terrible. Just awful! How could you make a call like that, Frank? You really blew it!"

The umpire let the coach have his say, and more. Then, in a quiet voice said, "Coach, you know I'm a lousy plate umpire and that I would blow the call. Why did you send your runner?"

The frustrated coach stared at the umpire for a moment and then said, "Good point!" The coach was Smitty.

Yes, we all make mistakes, including us coaches. But what do we require of our people in blue, while we coaches wear sunscreen and bask in the sunshine of perfection?

Let's see. Umpires should be on time, dress sharp, and be professional. That is a given. They should know the rules and work hard to make calls correct. Another given. They should take pride in their work and after the game study their methods, calls, and any mistakes in order to become better at their trade. That too should be a given, but we all know that there are those who are not given to givens.

We know some umpires are lazy and are in the game for the money. Some make no effort to learn the rules, and they are pompous and arrogant. Others care nothing about the game, the players, the fans, or the coaches. Some make bad calls continually and make no effort to improve.

On the other hand, most umpires work hard to do a good job. They try their best. They know the rules, or at least, most of them. Whatever mistakes are made, are honest ones. They deal with obnoxious people all the time, and in some games, they can do nothing right, according to some coaches and fans.

To indict umpires as a group is not very insightful, nor is it accurate. Were we to apply the same standards to our coaching, that is, be perfect, there wouldn't be any coaches.

Let's take the typical game, there being no such thing. A plate umpire may have to make several hundred decisions, many of which are easy. Some of these are: fair and foul, safe or out, ball and strike, hit batter, interference, obstruction, safety matters, in or out of play, batting out of order, obnoxious fans, on and on and on. And, of course, the umpire must always be right to the satisfaction of both sides.

The field umpire has it a bit easier, but not always. It seems the tough calls always occur when conditions are miserable, when everyone is tired, and when the game is very important to both sides. It is then that every play is close and satisfaction from coaches and fans does not often appear.

All coaches will say, "All I want from the umpires is that the calls should be correct and the strike zone consistent."

A noble generalization, but that is not what they mean. What they mean is, "Let's call the corners for my pitchers and make any close plays go my way. Also, don't make the strike zone too big when we're batting."

Perhaps this is a bit unfair to coaches, but think about it the next time you watch a game as an impartial observer. Listen to the coaching comments on close plays. Hear the moans when a pitcher "misses" on a pitch.

Umpires sometimes create their own problems, too. There are showboats out there who have to make a big production out of every call. They think the crowd came to see them umpire. Don't you just love it when a runner is out by 20 feet and in the very loudest of voices, the umpires goes, "Haaaaaaaaawwwwwwww!!!"? One would think they are attempting to regurgitate their suppers.

Then we have the "show me the ball" syndrome. This is where there is a close play, and the umpire hovers over the players groveling on the ground near a base. No call is made while the umpire screams, "Show me the ball!"

The fielder, obeying the command of the umpire, shows the ball, and the umpire jumps in the air screaming some unintelligible war cry signifying an out. This, while other runners are scampering about the bases. Don't you just love it?

The ruling bodies ordain that umpires should "sell the call" when the plays are close. This sets the stage for the actors, but it is Smitty's Law that if a call is correct, there is no need to sell it.

There are showboat coaches, too. These people want the world to know they are the boss. It is wonderful to see such coaches meet the arrogant umpires on the field. Sometimes, July 4th has fewer fireworks.

Improvement is needed in all aspects of the game. Less combat on the field of combat is needed, too, along with fairness, and an understanding of the roles of the other soldiers in the war. While heated discussions are bound to occur between coaches and umpires, let's try to keep it civil. Then, after it's over, it's over.

Cryin' the blues, however, is most definitely a lousy way to explain losses.

Chapter 57
SOFTBALL PLAY POTPOURRI

Situation Number One:

In a game played not too long ago, a runner was on first, with no one out, and the batter bunted. The second baseman stood like a statue as the pitcher fielded the ball and threw it to an imaginary player covering first base. This resulted in a wild throw into right field and a terrible conclusion.

The shortstop said to the second baseman, "Hey, I think you're supposed to cover first on a bunt."

The object of her comment stood motionless, sporting a blank stare.

The shortstop said, "Yeah, I mean…well. Oh, it's all so very confusing."

Translation: The shortstop would prefer someone at second base who knew how to play the position, or she would like the coach to train the current statue on the finer points of the game.

Situation Number Two:

Same game. Runners on first and third. Runner on first took off for second base. No play was made. The catcher did nothing except throw the ball back to the pitcher. The runner going to second was tempting the pitcher to throw the ball so that the third base runner could score. The second baseman and the shortstop stayed put. The pitcher was upset. She looked helplessly in the direction of the coach.

The coach said, "Don't get cute."

Glancing at the coach, the pitcher said, "But coach…"

Translation: The coach would prefer the pitcher to go about the business of pitching, because it would be stupid to make a play on the runner going to second. The pitcher would prefer to make a play, not wanting runners to indiscriminately waltz about the base paths. Her gaze at the coach suggested that the team should be prepared with some sort of play in this situation, rather than feebly standing about.

Situation Number Three:

In a recent game, the pitcher dashed to the mound after her teammate made the last out of the inning. No one else hustled onto the field, and she waited for a catcher. The coaches moseyed about while the reserve players lounged on the bench, chatting with parents and fans. The remainder of the team jogged at varying speeds to their respective positions. The pitcher watching in total disgust said, "Come on you guys! We've got a game to play."

Translation: The pitcher would have rather been home watching the grass grow. She wished she had joined a team that hustles. But, she is committed and will stay the year. Oh, well.

Situation Number Four:

Late in a game, lots of runs having been scored, both teams continued play in terrible fashion. A fielder came into the dugout after the third out of an inning and asked, "Won't this game ever end? I'm missing my T.V. program."

Translation: The player was bored and would rather be elsewhere. Why she joined the team is a mystery. She is nothing but aggravation, and all the other players agree that she should have been home watching her program.

Situation Number Five:

In a recent game, a runner attempted to steal, but was called out on a close play. The coach on offense was indeed offensive, maintaining that there was no tag. Curiously, his team was down 12 runs at the time. Excellent time to steal, eh?

After the game, the coach followed the umpire into the parking lot, shouting, "No tag. There wasn't a tag."

Just then the runner who had been called out happened by and said, "Coach, she tagged me."

Of course, this made the coach angrier and he proclaimed, "There may have been a tag on my runner, but the umpire was out of position and couldn't have seen it."

Translation: The coach was right even if he was wrong. So, there! It was clear that only umpires make mistakes. Coaches never do. Even if they get 10 runners thrown out, it only takes one questionable umpire call to negate the ten coaching "errors." Fault must flow to the umpire. It is an unwritten rule.

Situation Number Six:

This quandary is connected to the last. This occurred in a game where there had been many good calls by a particular umpire, but two that were very close and went against one of the teams. As the umpire made a call that went against the same team, the coach loudly proclaimed, "That's three, now!"

Translation: The umpire had "blown" three calls. But the umpire never got credit for the good calls. Even if later in the game, two close calls go the way of the "offended" coach, the ump's score will remain at three unless another bad call is made, in which case the score will soar to four. Our poor umps just never get out of the hole.

Situation Number Seven:

In another game, a new first baseman was in the act of fielding a batted ball with runners on second and third. Both runners broke. Did the fielder tag the batter; throw to the second baseman at first base; throw home; tag the batter and throw home; or just stand there?

The player did none of the above. She threw the ball to second base where there was no fielder, only the umpire, who was most certainly not expecting a play there. He dodged death as the ball whizzed past his head into the left-center field gap. All runners scored.

The coach asked in a tone that any discerning person would recognize, "What in the &%$$#$# were you doing?"

The player responded, "Coach, you always told us to be ready for a play after a play, so I was doing that."

"Doing what?"

"Making a play after a play."

"Yes, and?"

There was no response, but the coach said, "Well, I guess that explains that."

Translation: None.

There are some interesting moments on the field where the

great game of softball is played. All manner of conditions arise. Nothing is ever the same. The game is ever surprising and delightful. Anecdotes are in the zillions and present themselves to us on a daily basis. All we need is a good sense of humor and then seek the translations.

Chapter 58
WHATTA RIDE, PART II

Well, how do those "also in the running," the high school softballers who aren't being scouted, get a piece of the scholarship pie? How can we get a college coach to take a look at a kid who wants to play, is willing to work hard, has good grades, and has tremendous potential? The road is there, but it has many bumps, curves, and land mines. And in my opinion, it's a high school coach's duty to be able to impart some wisdom to his players who desire to play in college, even if they aren't Division I potential stars.

Let's assume most of this year's senior crop has been scouted and/or recruited. Those who haven't are still in the running, but the light grows dim with each passing day. Chances are that if Division I schools wanted them, they would have been in their living rooms already. But all is not lost. What applies to underclassmen can also apply to the current left-out bunch. So, what can be done to get someone to notice your players?

By all means, players should send a tape and personal information to any college that they might want to attend. They should visit the campus and talk to the coach. And they should have recommendations from coaches, teachers, or fans that are sent separately from their tape. Next the high school or summer coach, that's you coach, should call the college coach. And if all possible it behooves the young player to get the college coach to come out to see them play.

A college coach or scout will notice many things. All the players at a game will be scouted, not just the ones that the coach came to see. What is the scout thinking?

Look at that player! Is that the one who wrote or sent a tape? I came to this game to see someone else. She sprints to her position as fast as she can go. She returns to the bench in the same way, and has beaten all her teammates to the dugout. What hustle!

Forget the one I came to watch. I'm watching her, the one who hustles! Wow! She is the first one off the bench to chase foul balls, and she does it at full speed. When she is the on-deck batter, she races to pick up the last hitter's bat and, if necessary, gets into position to direct an incoming runner at the plate.

Fantastic! She hustles to the plate to bat, keeps one foot in the box to take signals, runs out all ground and fly balls at top speed, sprints to first base on walks, and alertly takes signals. And, is she ever aggressive at the plate! She attacks, attacks, and attacks, yet knows the strike zone. I've not seen her swing at a bad pitch. What discipline handling those risers and drops out of the strike zone.

And hit the ball down and hard? You bet! Didn't see one fly ball. She was on twice and scored once. She made a terrific pop-up slide at second base, and she did a fabulous fade-away slide at home. The catcher had no chance to get her.

Yeah, and she dropped down a drag bunt on her own, because the third baseman was cheating toward the bag. Beat it out, too!

It's clear someone has taught her how to run. Her arms pump hard, and she drives her elbows and legs. She's not the fastest player I've seen, but does she ever get a jump on the ball in the field and is she ever quick out of the batter's box.

But look at her on the bench, too! She is always watching the game. She's into every play. Other kids are jawing, including the kid I came to watch. But not her. If her team is on offense, she warns runners of pick-off plays, yells out the number of outs, and she constantly shouts encouragement. If not playing, she watches the opposing runners for missed bases. She warns if runners are advancing, stealing, or trying delay steals. She notices defenses, where the opposing pitcher is throwing to teammates. Yes, she is really into the game.

What game sense! She knows exactly what to do with the ball when she gets it. She is never at a loss to make a play. It is automatic, as if she anticipated every enemy move.

Listen to her talk to her teammates. There is no idle chatter. Everything she says pertains to the game. She talks about the wind, its direction and velocity. She moves her teammates around according to the batter's stance, build, apparent speed, and where she hit the ball last time up. What leadership!

There is no wasted motion in the field and no idleness between pitches. She is walking around, smoothing out the ground at her position, testing the wind, and keeping her arms and legs loose.

What an attitude! She works with the other players, not against them. She encourages them after they make a mistake and gets them to feel better about themselves. Then, when she makes a boo boo, she immediately picks herself up and gets back in the game. There is no pouting, no glove pounding, helmet throwing, or other tantrums.

To heck with the player I came to scout. I'm going to continue watching HER. Hey! Watch her fielding those grounders. What great technique. She charges the slow rollers and uses a great run-through throw, getting most of the runners. Her forehand and backhand techniques are superb.

Now, for some reason, they've moved her to the outfield. Look at that drop step. Notice how she works hard between innings on her practice throws. She's sure not lazy. She practices fly balls and grounders alike. She charges and goes back on balls. She never wants the practice fly or grounder thrown directly at her. What a work ethic!

Did you notice this kid between innings when her team came in? She was to be the fifth hitter, but she put on her helmet, walked behind the dugout, and began taking practice swings. She even had a little soft toss with herself where she would throw up a ball and hit it into the fence. And look! When she was like the seventh batter up during a time out, she picked up her glove and a ball, went behind the dugout, and did some drills on her own. I saw her working her glove on the bench, making it into sort of a basket. There sure aren't many errors in that glove. The glove is in fine condition just like she is.

You should have seen the pre-game activities. She led the team in running and stretches. She never just stood around. She was constantly working. Very impressive.

Her team went down by 10 runs. You'd have thought they were ahead from the way she acts. She never frowns, never argues, and never says anything to the umpire unless asked. She keeps pumping up her teammates, too. The game never ends for her.

Whenever the coach asks her to do something, she says, "Yes, coach." Then, she sprints to her appointed job. Guess who picks up the equipment after the game? She does. Thought that was the job of the underclassmen.

Grades? You bet! Her coach says she studies every night. Gets As and Bs. Wants to be a teacher. She'll make a good one, too. Do I want this kid on my team? You bet! And 17 more just like her.

So, can everything that impressed the coach be learned? Well, the Magic Tooth Fairy won't do it for your softballers, but hard work and a great desire to be good athletically and academically will. It might even get your player that "ride" to the school of her choice.

Chapter 59
LET'S TALK ABOUT THE WEATHER

Oh, Southern and Western crowds will cheer.
For their exquisite weather is extremely clear.
But there is no joy in Northland,
Dreary snow days draw ever near.

November is such a depressing month. Dreams of softball are dulled by the gathering gray clouds, accompanied by the ever-decreasing temperature, and they, in tandem, proclaim that if one wants to play softball, it better be indoors. We Nanooks of the North are stuck with our surroundings, while the Gloaters (those residing in the South and West) smirk and chuckle at our plight. Well, stop pouting and deal with it, for softball seasons will ever and anon be as they are today. This is just another Smitty editorial and has nothing whatsoever to do with the subject at hand, that being a look at what kids often do or don't receive from coaches.

It is Smitty's law that winning is the direct result of the correct execution of fundamentals. Willful disregard of this law is evident among many coaches who brazenly ignore the basics as a matter of routine and their records testify to the extent of their delinquencies. I would have these charlatans relegated to coaching nothing but a swarm of angry parents chosen from the most hypocritical of fans.

Just take a few moments to watch the "great" softball instruction going on in "T" ball at park districts, in volunteer organizations across our nation, and, yes, even during travel team and college practices and games. Those in charge may have their hearts in the right place and on the surface, at least, they mean well. However, they have no idea of the damage they are doing to players, mentally and physically, as well as to the game.

At the onset, Mom, Pop, guardian, or baby sitter brings little Suzie Notsogood, age nine, to the festivities two or three times a week during the summer months. She joins other kids who are often dropped off at the free baby sitting service for a couple of hours.

There is always the heavy set kid, the skinny kid, the brat, the kid with thick eyeglasses, maybe a mentally or physically handicapped kid, some kids who are slow, some who are fast, and some very athletic kids, along with the mayor's daughter. Interesting how the gifted ones and those with connections receive the most attention, while the less fortunate languish in a sea of neglect.

Youth coaches are mostly volunteers or paid municipal employees. Although there are those who are experienced in playing, there are few who are skilled in the niceties of the game. These coaches take Suzie and their other charges onto the diamond and hit a few grounders and fly balls. There is seldom any instruction, although one will hear such things as: "Don't drop the ball," or "Level swing, now," or "Don't take your eye off the ball," or "Nice try," or some other words of infinite wisdom on how to play the game.

When Suzie finally throws a ball near an intended receiver, who will promptly drop it, the "coach" will yell, "Way to throw the ball! What a cannon!" Cannon, indeed!

When preparing to bat, Suzie's small hands reach out for a bat that Godzilla would have trouble holding, much less wielding. She swings at the coach's lob balls by first dropping the bat to knee level, then swinging up, finally falling backwards. If she is strong, perhaps she will be able to swing the "tree" she is holding somewhere near the pitched ball, using a wide arm-swing. She may hit many beautiful, foul line drives, and after each one, coach will shout, "Way to hit the ball! Straighten it out!" But, of course, Suzie can't "straighten it out," because she doesn't know how.

Catching, throwing, and batting are the primary areas "covered" in these sessions. It is bad enough that the basics of each are generally not taught correctly. Ignored completely are sliding, base running, backhand, and forehand tosses, flip tosses, sacrifice and drag bunting, leadoffs, diving for balls, diving back to bases, rules of the game, and maybe, most importantly, how to protect oneself against the dangers of the game.

Dangers of the game? Yes, that ball can come at a fielder at tremendous speeds. Are kids taught how to avoid pitches thrown directly at them, how to slide correctly, how to tag a runner, all of which, if done incorrectly, can cause injury? There are many perils just waiting for the unwary on the diamond. It is not all fun and games when those flashing red lights appear on the horizon with their wailing accompaniment.

What is just as bad are the mental scars left by malignant coaching. There will never by any stats as to how many kids, gifted and otherwise, started playing softball, but quit when they were confronted with incompetence, arrogance, and pitiful instruction from us coaches.

But Suzie, along with some of the better athletes, may survive the early trials of mental and physical endurance. If she is lucky she will get some good coaches along the way who will try, with or without success, to remedy the harm done to her fundamentals. Only the very lucky go on to receive great coaching that advances their skills to the best of their abilities. The rest will be befuddled and confused by a variety of coaching skills and attitudes, even at the very highest levels of softball.

Now, where does all this lead and what can be done about it? Every program must find competent instructors who can teach the basics. If there are not enough, then the competent must instruct those unskilled in the fine art of coaching. Thereafter, they must provide supervision until the coaches can do it on their own. Some programs do this, or at least make a good attempt with varying results.

Usually not enough time is put into learning, and the coaches go onto the field with just enough knowledge to be dangerous. They may even know how to play the game very well, but knowing something and being able to teach it are two different things.

Unfortunately, there are some coaches who are very dangerous characters on the diamond. They are the "know-it-alls," who so often have no desire to learn or try anything new. Players who survive these types are the true champions of the game.

As with most things, knowledge about one's subject is a requisite if one is to succeed. But if one is to pass along this knowledge, one must also know how to teach it to others. Softball is no different.

Frankly, there are far too many young girls with arms so sore they can't throw a ball, knees in braces, and other injuries, many of which could have been prevented with proper coaching. Sickening too, is the vast number of kids who might have made it to the "big time" or even the "little time" had they been correctly instructed. Many of those who quit along the way often do so, not because of the lack of ability, but because of the blunders of others, mostly us adults.

Cold weather gives us Nanooks a great opportunity to do something about our abilities as coaches. We are given the time to study and learn. Hopefully, the more fortunate ones living in warm weather climes will do the same. Maybe this was all about weather, after all.

Chapter 60
ALL I WANT FOR CHRISTMAS

We all make wishes, mostly at Christmas. We make wishes all the time. There is no guarantee that they will come true, but we do it anyway. It makes us feel good.

Let's see what a softball player might wish for:

1. **A college softball scholarship, preferably a full ride**. I know they're out there, but that they are not as abundant as one might think. They are limited...very limited. Only the best get "full rides," and not many of them, at that. Money is scarce, and it may be that I won't qualify for any of it. By the way, I studied hard in school and got good grades, because I know that there's probably more money available for academic scholarships than for athletes. And, college coaches dearly love good students.

2. **A bat with lots of hits in it**. Hmmmmm, let's see. I want one like the one Marybellsue uses. Yeah! She gets lots of hits. I'll ask for one just like hers. One the other hand, maybe I should look for one with good balance and feel. I don't think a 35-inch, 33-ounce tree is good. I think I'd prefer a lighter bat, one, say 33 inches long, weighing 25 ounces, because it is lighter and gives me more bat speed. I want the bat to be tapered and thin, so that I can get a good grip up in the fingers, good wrist action, and quickness. Yes, I'll get a bat that's suitable for me and not one simply because it is fashionable.

3. **A glove that doesn't make errors**. Maybe if I practiced with the one I've got and used good technique, I wouldn't need a new one, but gosh, the one I have is old and beat up. But if I get a new one, I'd want it to fit my hand, one of that I can feel the ball in, one that's soft and broken in, not one of those humongous ones that are heavy, and in which I always lose the ball. Maybe too, if I get a new glove, I'll

take care of it. I'll wipe it off with a damp rag, outside and inside, and then apply a good softening agent. Which agent? I'll ask our little old shoemaker. Such people deal with leather all the time and will give me good advice. The stuff I've been using might rot the leather and not help it. Oh yeah, if I take care of my glove, it is a fact that I'll make at least 10 percent fewer errors.

4. **A snazzy uniform with big numbers and my name on it**. After all, these things give me a high profile and surely make me play better. But that's not really so, and I have to remember that people will also see my name when I do badly. A nice appearing uniform, worn properly, with any size number on it will do nicely. If I have talent, not to worry. I'll be recognized by the right people.

5. **A coach that will teach me**. Yes, I want a coach who will give me good instruction, discipline, fairness, and love. Coach will show me the right way to do things, and if he/ she doesn't know, will find someone that can. And please, coach, if I need a dressing down, you needn't scream. Just do it in a firm voice, with conviction, so that I will understand what is needed. If I get that, I will respond.

6. **A decent field, free from mole holes and dangerous obstacles**. And get me one that is well-maintained. Heck, I'll drag it myself if I can get the equipment.

7. **A colossal amount of understanding and patience from my parents**. They need to know I am young and will make mistakes. They need to encourage me all the time and always be positive. Please!

8. **Discipline**. I must be strong, work hard, dress correctly, be on time, be faithful to my coach and my team, tell others to lay off the criticism of my fellow players and/or coach, uphold the traditions of my team, and otherwise be dedicated to the principles of fair play and the game.

9. **Courage**. Yes, I need courage to admit when I'm wrong and not blame others. I need the courage to handle a chewing out by the coach and to understand that coach is only trying to help me and does not mean things personally.

10. **Fun**. Lots and lots of fun on the field. Give me that, plus love and instruction, and I will perform beyond my coach's wildest dreams. This is one of the things that will bring me back next year.

A coach might ask for:

1. **Positive kids who want to learn**. Enough of these brats who go out for softball just for something to do and don't care about learning or working hard. I want kids who want to play and will run through a brick wall for the team. "Brick Wall" kids, I cleverly call them. Oh yeah, keep the prima donnas on some other team. Let them start every game at their favorite positions and give some other coach grief. I don't want it.

2. **Some help**. Yes, I need someone to help me maintain the field, raise money, practice the kids, make calls, carry equipment, and tons of other stuff.

3. **A money tree**. 'Nuf said.

4. **Good umps**. Almost enough said, but Santa has to bring me some patience too, for umps are not always as perfect as I am. They are human, make mistakes, and I must understand this, even in the heat of battle when a "bad" call hurts my team.

5. **Understanding parents**. As a coach, I will try my best, but I need support from parents. I'll make lots of mistakes, have poor lineups, bad strategy, and may be negative at times, but I need parents who will back me up, and not go around backbiting me. Heck, if parents have concerns or a criticism, let them come talk to me. We can work most things out.

6. **I need some understanding, too**. I must get some patience. I must realize that I am a teacher and know that whatever I do, whether good or bad, will affect the kids. I must lead them in the right direction. Heaven knows, today's world is full of the wrong directions, so I need to make a good, solid, and positive impact on my team.

7. **Fortitude to admit when I'm wrong**. This is a tough thing

for a coach to do. It may be the toughest task in coaching, but it must be done. I need lots and lots of courage, for there are many times when things go wrong, and I must stand up and do what's right.

Wish lists can go on forever, whether it be for Christmas or otherwise. Coaches want the best for their teams, and the players want the best for themselves and their team. It is not much of a mystery, all this. It is what everybody wants from the game, or for that matter, from life...just a fair opportunity.

Chapter 61
IF I WERE KING...

If I were king, well, I'd do some interesting stuff regarding softball. No, I wouldn't alter the game much. It's pretty good the way it is, but there are a few things my subjects would have to endure that heretofore have not been mandated. Let's check it out.

First, I would establish a punishment. This would be banishment to the Softball Nether Outer World (SNOW), which is a place of eternal rain, cold, and snow, where all the softball diamonds are made of solid granite, and one must listen incessantly to gurus who claim to know everything about everything. Ugh! What a place!

Rule makers would go to SNOW right away, because they won't change the high school and college softball seasons to the fall. Once they were gone, I would immediately change things. Following the rule makers would be those who coach and administrate in the South and West. They think only of the advantage they have over the rest of the country with the current status quo and care not that the playing field would be leveled were the playing seasons changed. This would be my first act as sovereign.

I would banish hard bases to SNOW along with the ogres already noted. I wonder how many ankles and knees have been injured on bases when one runs over them or slides into them. It would seem that softer bases, with give, would make sense. Although they are manufactured, precious few are used. Breakaway bases are good too, because they move when contacted by sliding players. However, they, too, are hard, so I would edict that softer bases be used.

There are home plates all over the place that, when wet, provide skating rink like surfaces for kids as they race to score. Scores of kids are unnecessarily injured at these times. There are non-skid bases available, so I'd edict that they be placed in position immediately on all diamonds.

I'd ordain that all on-deck batters remain behind the hitter, regardless of which dugout their team inhabits. Batters whose stance is open to kids waiting to hit often hit sharp foul balls, and being struck by one is not a lot of fun. The problem is easily eliminated, but our rule makers ignore the obvious.

If I were king, I'd make kids keep their helmets on when running bases. In case you haven't noticed, the softball game is such that a thrown ball and a runner often have the same destination and frequently arrive at the same time. Since a thrown ball can provide as much damage as a pitch, it would seem prudent to prohibit runners from removing their protection. Maybe chin strips would help those who say, "But, gosh, my helmet just comes off when I run." It's only logical.

Now, in my realm, I have observed kids taking a pitch in the face. They catch it there, too, sometimes when the ball comes off the bat in an eerie sort of way. This latter event sometimes occurs when bunting, principally because the bat is held too far away from the head. We must protect the unwary, for we need them in the lineup, and we want them as healthy after the game as they were before. The solution is simply to put a football-style face guard on the helmet. Actually, a simple bar would suffice. The bar, of course, is not cool, but if we continue to leave it off, players can become cool when they put the ice packs on their swollen noses after being bonked by a ball.

I'd prohibit a batter from deliberately throwing a bat into fair territory after bunting. It is so easy to retain a bat and flip it out of harms way after hitting a ball. But the rules allow bunters to literally fling it toward oncoming fielders. Not nice. Lefty slappers are the most guilty of this delinquency. Such nonsense!

I'd dispatch many park district bosses and field maintenance overlords to SNOW for their failure to put safety guards on the top of those chain-link fences around ball diamonds. While trying to catch a ball, kids often get whacked on one of those little metal projections on top of these fences. Makes for a nice wound. There are plastic gizmos, cheap ones too, that should be on top of all chain-link fences. Yes, I'd require those. Tennis balls are cheap. One can cut a slit in a tennis ball and put it on top of those spears holding up temporary fences around softball diamonds. I'd sure hate to see a kid fall into one of those deadly items. People who allow this delinquency would be expressed to SNOW in a heartbeat.

Then, too, how about those chain link fences with curled-up bottoms that make wonderful traps for feet? Don't suppose anyone has ever seen a kid's foot entangled in this manner, eh? Well, I have and it ain't pretty.

Regarding rule changes, I would demand that the obstruction be redefined to absolutely, positively, and forever prohibit a fielder, including a catcher, from blocking a base. Since one may not deliberately crash into a player when trying to get to a base, it is difficult to explain to a runner what to do when approaching an armored warrior, posing as a catcher, completely blocking access to home plate. Slide around? Oh, sure, and get called for being out of the baseline. Slide hard into the blocker? Oh, sure, and come off short of the plate, all the while risking potentially enormous harm to both runner and blocker. Some answer! Banishment, I say! Begone to SNOW, ye nincompoops who have failed to recognize the problem.

There is no one thing loathed by all more than the International Tie Breaker Rule. It is so wonderful to struggle and struggle in a tough game between two determined opponents, and then have the people in blue tell you to put a runner on second base for the tie breaker. Gone with ye! I'd send the rule to SNOW along with the person who devised it, set up a tie game, and edict that no one would score for an eternity.

Then there are those coaches who put their personal interests above those of any player or the team as a whole. They sometimes lie to the kids, treat them unfairly, scream and yell constantly, never coach, and are always on the defensive about their lack of coaching ability. These people are gone...you hear? Gone!

Now, then, if I were king...I'd, well, I'd do lots more. But first I'd look in the mirror each day to make sure that I had not been dethroned. Next, since I hate playing in the cold, I would ask myself whether any of my grievances pertained to me.

Ah, if I were king...

Addendum
"DRAZ"

Robert "Draz" Drazkowski was a cigarette-smoking, worn-out, newspaperman from the "old school," having worked for numerous fourth estate enterprises. He "hunted and pecked" on a typewriter, feeling that computers are somehow responsible for the woes of mankind. He sneered at those media types who fail to report the truth, especially sports writers who coddle players, owners, and agents, hoping they will be favored with scoops. His background was forged during the "medieval" times of baseball, although he hammered on the anvil of most other sports, as well. He was a true expert and student of sports, especially baseball, having rubbed noses with some of the greats. He assisted me in the compilation of this "masterpiece," making voracious comments in the margins of the manuscript. They were numerous...too numerous to include in this work. Here are a few of them.

On success and the idea that there is only one winner at the end of every season: *In head-to-head competition, there's one winner and one loser. Carrying it a step further, the popular tournament formats of today produce a bevy of so-called "losers," but does that mean they have not been successful?*

Again, on success: *Attitude should always be an overriding factor. Regardless the team sport, success can't be spawned from the number one. Eleven is the number in football, five in basketball, and, of course, nine in baseball or softball. One piece in the puzzle never provides a true picture, and, in victory or defeat, the game should be a shared experience, the joy of unified effort.*

On warming up: *Running facilitates a sweat, loosens the entire body, but you don't see it much these days.*

Regarding the bag at first base: *There should be a safety base for all youth and high school games.*

On injuries: *They deplete bench personnel and affect strategic moves.*

On sliding during steals: *Players should slide to the infield side, because more and more shortstops are taking throws behind the bag.*

On big leadoffs at second base: *A strong lead is bothersome to the shortstop's sight lines and is a distraction.*

On aggressive base running: *The pitcher's thinking is influenced by aggressive base running, because it causes a distraction and tests the pitcher's confidence.*

On hitting: *Too often, I think, hitters create their own "hitting zone," rather than going with the eye-to-ball concept, creating their own distinct blind spot.*

The hours spent with Draz were not only golden, but added to the knowledge and character of anyone fortunate enough to have the opportunity to be with him. The world lost him recently and with his passing a true friend.

About the Author

Dick Smith (Smitty) has been active in softball and baseball as a player, coach, and umpire for over sixty years. He has coached all ages of girls and boys from tiny tots to women's teams. From the fall of 1984 to the spring of 1994, he guided the Lady Saints softball team from the University of St. Francis, Joliet, Illinois to national prominence. From the fall of 1994 to the spring of 1996, he was head coach at Valparaiso University. He returned to St. Francis as an assistant coach in the fall of 1996 and has since taken over the helm of the team. Smith is a popular clinic speaker and a noted instructor, having appeared at several national and local clinics. Softball represents a full-time pursuit for Smith since his retirement from government service. He and his wife, Ruth, reside in Illinois. They have two children, Ernie and Tracy.